MILLIONAIRES
ARE PROPITIOUS
&
BILLIONAIRES
ARE PERFORMERS

What It Takes to Become a Masterpiece

DR. SAN BHARATH

INDIA • SINGAPORE • MALAYSIA

Notion Press

No.8, 3rd Cross Street, CIT Colony,
Mylapore, Chennai,
Tamil Nadu – 600004

First Published by Notion Press 2020
Copyright © Dr. San Bharath 2020
All Rights Reserved.

ISBN 978-1-63606-717-9

This book has been published with all efforts taken to make the material error-free after the consent of the author. However, the author and the publisher do not assume and hereby disclaim any liability to any party for any loss, damage, or disruption caused by errors or omissions, whether such errors or omissions result from negligence, accident, or any other cause.

While every effort has been made to avoid any mistake or omission, this publication is being sold on the condition and understanding that neither the author nor the publishers or printers would be liable in any manner to any person by reason of any mistake or omission in this publication or for any action taken or omitted to be taken or advice rendered or accepted on the basis of this work. For any defect in printing or binding the publishers will be liable only to replace the defective copy by another copy of this work then available.

This book was intentionally not for an ordinary life's, it's only for whom, want to become a MASTERPIECE

You can become a millionaire in 6months just by creating a PROPITIOUS CIRCUMSTANCE & you just need to work there;

But for becoming a billionaire you need to create a GRIM CIRCUMSTANCE & perform like a masterpiece!

This book is dedicated to

Unrelieved intimacy of my beloved

Dr. Haritha Srinivas

And

Dr. Bhaskar Srojan

— Dr. San Bharath

My Special thanks for the great personalities who left their footprints in my mind, and allowed me to think;

- ✓ Bheemanna lakshmi Bai
- ✓ M Vasantha Chatra Naik
- ✓ Narayana K. C
- ✓ Dr. P. Murali mohan
- ✓ Dr. A.K Jeelani
- ✓ Dr. Madhu
- ✓ Dr. Uma Maheshwari
- ✓ Dr. SrinivasRadha
- ✓ Ln Dr. Prabhakar V
- ✓ Ln D Madhu Mohan
- ✓ Ln Y Prabhakar Naidu

Contents

Introduction 13

My Prayer 17

Chapter 1   ...Knowing Your Power

    Life Is? 21

    Live In Present 25

    Find Your End 30

    Dreams, Goals and Desires 34

    Be a Dream Driven 39

    Desire as Passion 45

    Understanding mind, knowing intention and reason! 50

    Rational and Irrational Influence 55

    Life is by thinking 60

    Developing a Rational Mindset with Epistemology 64

Contents

Chapter 2   Divinity and Reality

Selfishness is the Divinity of Life 72

Selfishness is breath of every Human 77

Jealousy and Profitability; 81

Never depend too much on others; It means don't trust anyone Irrationally 86

Fear is Just Your Illusion, Fear Lives until You Understand that Illusion 89

A Reason of Surrender 92

Time is Irreversible Gift 98

Live in Recluse at least 30 min a day 105

Break the emotion which Breaks you 109

Break the Hurts and Sufferings 114

Self Made Man 119

The Power 129

Chapter 3   Propitious Circumstance

If you want to become the worst possibility you can become a millionaire with 1% of your potential 144

Propitious Circumstance 148

Don't stay with loss & don't stop with Richness 152

Concept of Money 156

Money Is Not an Evil; Lack of Money is an Evil 160

Time Eater is Poor and Time Utilizer is Rich 168

Living without Money? 171

It's your Right to be Rich 175

You Can't Get a Successful Life Unless You Are Rich 181

Becoming a Millionaire 184

To Sell (Or) To Be Sold 191

6 Months Formula 195

Financial Freedom Has No Shortcuts It Has a Formula 198

Perception of Network Marketing or M.L.M 203

Strong Image Will Receive More Richness 216

A lesson from a Death Bed 221

Chapter 4   Grim Circumstance

Become a Masterpiece by Getting Control over Yourself 229

Grim Circumstance 253

World is Made ny Few Performers, Aren't You a Performer? 257

The Cultured Education for a Billionaire 261

Building a Master Piece Mindset 264

The Billionaire Formula 270

Introduction

"Life is either projecting to an enthusiastic joy or dragging into excitement by learning". Life is nothing, if you don't have both enthusiasm & excitement.

– Dr. San Bharath

Ultimate purpose of life is fulfilling our life. Fulfillment of life doesn't come just with money & angriness; along with richness, you must have the time, power, a passion towards the purpose of life – and it's more than what I ever known about life.

I failed more than 48times in finishing & publishing this book from many months. But at that moment I excused myself with: I was busy in my profession, and industrial unit work; but didn't finish this book only due to my ignorance.

After few days I have nothing, such things in my mind to fulfill in this life, because I fulfilled all my basic needs and dreams which I want to do in my life. By profession I am Doctor, became CEO to our company in small age. I lost interest and excitement in earning and spending money & more, my life became boredom.

I started roaming places, which too didn't help me in removing my loneliness & bore feeling from my life. Many times I held up with many questions, why I am still living without any cause & reason, I turned like a person who don't know how & why to live this life. I lost hope on life & fear on death. But I want to find the answers to my questions, which made me a rationalist by thinking about a reason & I became a thinker without my notice.

Philosophy has power to make you anything, it made me happy, it kept me excited, it removed my singleness & it helped me to lead again a new life by removing my unknown pains & introduced to new fulfillments, philosophy helped me to live & it gave me rebirth.

Before I know about philosophy, when I go to any library I use to see only medical book block & the fiction – nonfiction books & many new articles on human health. I never read about god & spiritual/philosophy books in my past. I thought philosophy is for weak peoples who doesn't know the value of life etc, but when life forced me to move into a philosophical world, I came to address the loss which I lost with my ignorance. This stage made me to read philosophy & live in philosophy. Philosophy made me Rich in all.

I wondered myself, to my Question- *"how to live & why to live without excitement and happiness in life"?* Was changed as:

"How worst I lived without philosophy"?

My proudest support was money; I dare to everything because I am rich! Iam like a person, Richness was my answer for every Question and money is the answer & language for all works; yet this is true for ever, I believe this even now & ever; this answer was end up with - "What richness I Earned - just money"? Earning Just money can really makes me rich? NO!

Money is the first priority in life, yes! Along with the money, yet more things were needed for living a complete life;

With this mindset, I came across the PROPITIOUS CIRCUMSTANCE and the GRIM CIRCUMSTANCE. I came to get clear understanding about the formulas of money and becoming a millionaire in just 6months, It's a practically proven formula for me, and it can be applicable to anyone, if they want to become a millionaire and doesn't want to limit their possibilities to live an ordinary life;

The transformation from grim circumstance can make you a masterpiece!

My Prayer

God,

Please Provide

Peace & Love To The Mankind,

Let Them Raise Not From Their Situation Of Darkness, But From Their Understanding And Reasoning Thinking...

Allow the Mankind to Think About Their Lives,

Don't Let Their Thinking Struck At Some Deadly End,

Show Them A Way, By Raising A Thought In Their Mind Towards Life.

Dreams, Goals &Needs Are To Be Fulfill
For Getting Most Enjoyable, Joyful, Meaningful
and Purposeful Life on This Earth

Desire Is The Something Which Creates Sufferings
In Your Life, On Reaching Your Destination Point
You Will Be Remained As Desire-Free Man On
This World.

– Dr. San Bharath

...Knowing Your Power

The Purpose of My Life

Nature became one and gave life to me, allowed me and placed me on this planet and gave everything for fulfilling the purpose of my life

iam born to fulfill the purpose of my life..

Iam living...

To reach all my dreams and desires which are mean to fulfill the purpose of my life

To kill all the fears and emotional disturbances which are obstricles to fulfill the purpose of my life

To serve all the living animals and plants which are serving me to live for fulfilling the purpose of my life

To develop all the knowledge to enlight peoples, who all supports me in making a move to fulfill the purpose of my life

To not cause any harm to myself and to others during the journey of fulfilling the purpose of my life

To beg an apology from all the mankind and nature to forgive me for any mistake in fulfilling the purpose of my life

To make meaning for my life while fulfilling the purpose of my life

To fulfill the purpose of my life...

– Dr. San Bharath

01

Life Is?

Life is not of just getting sugar, shelter & sex.

– Dr. San Bharath

"*Life is an Ego*, which was connected between the atom & the Energy". The ego holds emotions, excitement, enthusiasm, and more extra energies. I am called as living, when my ego was hold to the energies; if my ego shows only link to my atoms & not to energy then I am called energy dead & physical alive; if my ego was disconnected to my atom & connected to my energy, then it is called physical dead & energy alive; when the ego disconnects with both the atom & energy then it is called as complete Dead!

What you are? Are you living fully or partially or dead? I can see many people's around me who are living but not living, just alive; I can see no emotions, excitement, enthusiastic energies in their thoughts & acts. Some people we can see around us they are dead physically, but still they are living by their energy, by their performance made while they are living.

The energy which you hold to your ego is in the form of memory/ knowledge; you are what your memory is! You are called ever living until you keep gaining new knowledge by learning new things & more.

The energy which you hold to your ego was to live your life, not to waste your life for anyone else in your life as a sacrifice for the selfishness of peoples, don't expect any help for any human being; the help may be pressure as they feel or trouble they face; or the help may be commercial to them, don't lit a fire of pressure or pollution in someone's life.

You are born with all your capabilities to live your life in a great way; don't except any favor from anyone& don't accept any favour for anyone & don't waste your time in helping the un-needy; This will just create disturbances or destroys the relation between you & other.

Every challenge is an excitement & great education in your life, don't skip the excitement & joy from your life, by skipping the challenge with someone's help; accept your own challenge in your life, because you are born to face & open all the challenges which you deserve, if you take anyone's assistance, you lose the thrill, joy and mostly you will lose yourself and your capability may minimize!

> *"Your time is limited, so don't waste it living someone else's life. Don't be trapped by dogma – which is living with the results of other people's thinking."*
>
> *– Steve Jobs*

How big problem you get in your life?

Remember 37 trillion of cells (atoms) are there to stand with you & you don't need some other help to support you. You are born with the capability to solve and overcome your situations & trouble; No one will try seriously to lose their life and live for you, except your. If you want to move longer & greater life, you have to move alone; "this is your life –Your life is of your energy, your enthusiasm, your ego, & your 37 trillions of cells – keep a look on this & protect them in every situation, this is your basic responsibility of your body".

Human life is worst living on the earth, but we have born so we have to lead until our turn was over on this earth. We should not compromise with ourselves, there are no enemies to you by birth, and you are not born as someone's enemy, but the situations may create enmity among two.

The purpose of life is definitely not the enmity with others, so a man should compromise, ignore, neglect the situations and ask forgiveness to the rivalry with other, so that you will not disturb others life & you are not been disturbed by others in your life. You can use your memory, energy, enthusiasm, excitement in living your own life.

The best situation in the worst life was, letting the society to live your own life without any disturbance to you. It is most adventurous thing to live life without facing any difficulties, disturbances, insults & hurting in the life. Life is mean to yourself, but the society was formed by some people's fears & incompetence to live alone, so they formed to live in support & togetherness; and for living in the society, they crafted some responsibilities & rules; but these were making you to be as a dust particle in a blowing wind. The life is moving, in a wind; life is becoming very ordinary by being as and among society.

Let the society don't burglary you

A thief can show you a knife or a gun to steal something which you have, but such theft is not an actual harmful, Painful or destructive; but a LURKING BURGLARY can destruct you more than anything else;

It can damage your ideology, down your courage, can blind's your pathway, end-your dreams into a deadly desert, Break your will into fragment, it can fear you, it can make you alone into a deadly dark forest, t can leave you mid-way in the ocean of conflict, it can grave your potential, It will finally makes you as corpse.

You are conquered by society influence, you are born as original with extreme power & potential, but you will live a Ordinary life with broken Will's and Lost originality; this is happening by Lurking Burglary, your circumstance, people around you made you an like them by their influence on you, and making you to lose your true identity!

Such a dangerous thing this was, if you can escape from this Lurking burglary, undoubtedly can become a great personality on this earth.

This is the most complicated topic I felt to explain in a simple format for making you understand as it was utmost important for you to know the truth, I tried most not to hurt you emotionally with this fact-

"The influence of your friends, close circuit, family and your circumstance making you like them & killing your originality without your notice, you are losing yourself & your greatness, as a lion losing its nature and living as a grass eater by growing in sheep group, better find your originality at least now"

Life is became an employment, life is became a money earning process, life is became a cheating procedure; life is became worst or worst! Man made this culture of worseness, every human is moving in this way. "I can see many people whose has changed their life very dirtily for their company, the whole day & night life is for salaries & extra bonus. "In addition to this, the technology is spacing a great gap between you and your life".

But where we find this, in reality —*"Life is an Ego, which was connected between the atom & the Energy". Live your life greatly, let not go to a deadly desert end by someone's influence!*

02

Live In Present

"Living in the present with consciousness is most valuable and enjoyable moment equal to sex"

– Dr. San Bharath

If you are a person waiting for a right time to do your Work, You can never make that Work, because there is no abundant time for you, you have very limited time for you and which is not don't divide it as good & bad; the time to too less for every one of us, we should use all the knowledge, experience, support and utilize the Present Time and Live in every moment.

Dream Later, Do Actions Now! There is no excess Time, to Waste it! You can dream about your Future in Future & you Might have dreamed more than the required dreams in the past, now it's the time for your Action!

You have Exactly limited time than you can ever imagined about your time to make the things happen; Never waste the time which is like an non-renewable resource;

- *Spend More Time On The Great Ideas & Great Ideologies Which Can Make Your Life More Meaningful.*

- *Spend Very Less Time On The Incidents Happened & Relative Emotions Regarding The Incidents.*

- *Do Not Waste Your Time By Spending In Worrying, In Discussion About Others And By Fretting About Use Less Topics.*

- *Don't spend your time pricelessly in anyway, respect your time it must be worthy! Don't waste today which you can never get this day again.*

The Size of our dream or task are not the measure of the time we have in our life, but it's the measure of the action what we have do today in utilizing the time; How Big size of actions you can do today in making the dream true & achieving the task as early as possible! What Dare Action you can Make today in making your dream achievable with the time you left over. Live today in making action which are Most Useful for your life and postpone the other less useful tasks for tomorrow, Spend today for most Useful Works!

> *"No one saves us but ourselves. No one can and no one may. We ourselves must walk the path."*
>
> *– Gautama Buddha*

Use all the possible ways you have in achieving all your Dreams as early as possible, dare to leave which is necessary to leave which can distract you. Multiply the Work with all the possibilities you can do the best up to your knowledge, if you don't have such knowledge hire someone else with knowledge or get the knowledge first, but don't waste time uselessly.

Challenge yourself to become just 1% better today than your yesterday with the time you have today, gain 1% more knowledge today, do 1% more progressive work today, move 1% ahead more closer to your dream today, Make Sure by the end of the day, you became 1% more Better today in all the possible ways you can perform! Win your challenge today over your yesterday! Repeat this Challenge Everyday as you do today!

It's Possible! I made this, and all the successful peoples made it possible; "it was made by every successful person on the earth, not because they are successful but they made this so they are Successful". You can also make this, it's Possible!

"The future starts today, not tomorrow."

– Pope John Paul II

What is that you want to do in your life, are you doing that today?

Everyone wants to do something, to achieve some great things in their life; in such way, what you want to do in your life? Make sure that what you want to do, keep a list. Remove the unnecessary things first in the list & keep all the necessary things in the list!

Prior the most importance & emergency list first, there is no need to keep only single priority; you can keep any number of priorities, but only if that work carries a true & great importance in your life.

Now the Question is: Are You Doing That Today? Are you doing the work which is helping you progressive to move towards your wants or not?

If the work you are doing today is not supportive or non progressive to your Wants from any means, just leave that work & do the work which can bring your wants into reality! Don't ignore to do action today!

You are totally responsible for your achievement & accomplishments in your life. If you don't take responsibility today to move a step ahead in achieving your accomplishments, you can never see yourself as Successful in your life. A successful life is made by moves & actions of many TODAY'S, towards the achievement, if you ignore to do your possible action, today; forget about your success, tomorrow!

"There is only one day in your life i.e., TODAY", you can never get tomorrow in your life; don't think about Tomorrow, Work today! Keep all your possible Effort today! And make your step ahead towards your wants! Take total responsibilities of Every TODAY'S in your life; don't let it go waste by involving day with unnecessary things or works!

"Enjoy today with your most prior important, progressive work, and let postpone the other unnecessary entertainments to tomorrow". Enjoy today each & every movements you do towards your achievement, because this is the only day which you can do work for your success. From tomorrow you can enjoy other entertainments in your life.

"If you are depressed, you are living in the past, if you are anxious, you are living in the future, if you are at peace, you are living in the present."

– Lao Tzu

Are you achieving your dreams & goals? Achieving today?

"Living in the moment means letting go of the past and not waiting for the future. It means living your life consciously, aware that each moment you breath is a gift."

– Oprah Winfrey

The dreams or goals can never get achieved in a single day; they can be getting with the satisfaction of many days. When you satisfy the process of achieving your dreams, then you can definitely enjoy every step of achievement & one fine day it becomes true! Achieving a dream can be happen every day, suppose the Dream is of reaching 100steps, you can't jump it once, you have to move one step at a day and here every day you will achieve a part of dream, so every day you can be successful and you can enjoy every day for your success.

Try to make satisfy yourself with the Great Big Action you did today for fulfilling your desire, make a Great Big Action (GBA) stop not until you get satisfied today with the work you have Done! Irrespective of the result, you should get satisfaction with the work you have done!

To fulfill all your desire, the needy Prerequisite is, a desire to learn the required information & to adopt self with new Knowledge& willing to apply the gained knowledge in the required Spot. If you get the required Information & knowledge which is needy every day, you can definitely achieve your dream a part into reality every day; one fine day, the achievement will end by reaching it completely.

"There are only two days in the year that nothing can be done. One is called yesterday and the other is called tomorrow, so today is the right days to love, believe, do and mostly live."

– Dalai Lama

03

Find Your End

"Life without knowing destination is same as doing sex without a pleasure end, you get no interest anymore"

– Dr. San Bharath

The end is the destination point where you want to go; without knowing your destination you will remain roaming in pathless way, where you may miss the meaning and the value to your life.

It is most necessary and important to find your end (home) to where the journey of your life is & for? Your destination end will decide the pathway of your life. Be particular and clear about the destination home you want to reach by your journey. The destination should be unchangeable, please choose the destination clearly and confidently irrespective of that home, no matter where it is and how far from you. Choose the end (home) where your life is to be moved. I chosen for National Award, Yes my destination home to reach the National Award for my life, irrespective of my place and position, I decided this when I am 13. No matter what, I became a doctor, I became an author, I became an entrepreneur, and I am becoming an inventor too. No matter, what I do. But my destination was to reach my home for this life.

"Stubborn to your end (home), but not to the pathways or methods you reach your home. I am stubborn to my end (home) to go National Award, and my methods and pathways were too flexible, I may change the pathways of my journey according to my possibilities, but I am not flexible to change my end".

Identify your life's destination

The destination point is the place where you want to be; no matter you may also fix to go to mars planet, as Elon Musk was making his destination to move to Mars planet. But make sure to be ready for your journey, your journey will be based on your destination point (home). If you choose the wrong path, you may waste your valuable life time which can be irreversible. If you don't have a destination point to your life, your journey will be miserable.

So, "Choose your destination with your total consciousness and with reasoning to yourself. The reasoning may be by the influence of your past experience, your knowledge, your possibilities, your interest and your passion". When you choose and decide your destination point, your life will be driven by the force called Purpose which can drive you to your destination.

> *"If you have a strong purpose in life, you don't have to be pushed. Your passion will drive you there."*
>
> *– Roy T. Bennett*

Many people doesn't have a destination point for their life, so they will not be driven by their inner force, they will be pushed according to the outer wind called situation. No one can escape from death, no matter wherever they hide; one day everyone has to die this is unchangeable law of nature. In the same way, if you have a destination end, no matter who ever you are, you will be driven by your inner force called Purpose; likewise no matter whomever, the one without destination point can never reach his destination in his life, the value and purpose of life becomes meaningless.

Be a purpose driven man and live a valuable and meaningful life, not a situational driven. Man goes nowhere, when he doesn't know where to go. All the successful peoples are purpose driven towards their destination point, all the failure were not having destination, so they perish in poverty!

What you want to make with this life: A purpose driven, with a destination point which increases the value and meaningfulness to your life or to perish in poverty?

What is your success: _____!

What is your end Point: _____!

Think and decide; your total life will be based on this decision.

> "Nothing is more creative… or destructive…
> Than a brilliant mind with a purpose."
>
> – Dan Brown, Inferno

Burning desire to reach your end (home)

Be clear with the reason WHY? Why you decided your destination point, by reaching that destination point what will you get as a result? Think consistently about the result what you get when you reach your destination point.

Be clear about:

- ✓ Where you want to go (your destination point).
- ✓ Why you want to reach that point.
- ✓ What you get in your destination point (Result).

Write this on paper,

- ✓ Where: _____
- ✓ Why: _____
- ✓ Result: _____

I believe no other motivation is required for you, more than a clarity and understanding about your destination point. If you know where to go and why you should go, no other obstruction can be left on this earth to stop you, than yourself. So make yourself to be consistence with your destination point by doing a small practice below regularly:

- ✓ *Wright your destination point daily on a paper,*
- ✓ *Think once immediately when you wake up in the morning,*
- ✓ *Think a while what can you do now, to move closer to your home.*
- ✓ *Before sleep again see that destination point and observe what you did today, and what other necessary methods you have to do by tomorrow.*
- ✓ *See how far, you are from your home, draw an imaginary map on a paper.*
- ✓ *Keep a time table for your life, as you practiced in your school*

"He who has a way to live for can bear almost anyhow."

– *Friedrich Nietzsche*

04

Dreams, Goals and Desires

"Understanding something & moving in a Progressive way towards the destination, is more enjoyable moment a man can perceive better than Sex"

– Dr. San Bharath

The destination point is different than your dreams, goals and desires. The destination point is ultimate end of your life that should be the highest achievement of your life.

- ✓ The destination point is the maximum highest point (the purpose of life)
- ✓ Next to that you get Dreams,
- ✓ Next to dreams, you get goals,
- ✓ Next to goals you get desire and wants.

For understanding the Desire, you need to understand Want and Need difference.

Need Vs Want Vs Desire

Need – *it require, because it is essential or very important rather than just desirable.*

Want – *have a desire to possess or do; wish for.*

Desire – *desire can be defined as bigger want; a desire is more intense craving that a person has for something or someone. Desire is a stronger and intense feeling than a want.*

Knowing In Depth about Need & Desire

Need is totally personal to an individual. Need is the most essential and important rather than desire or wants.

Desire and want are something different than need, it is not based on personal or individual; desire and wants are for external one and it was impacted and influenced by external force. Desires are things or materials, moments that desperately wants in the future, Example: I desire to buy a Rolls Royce car in Future. "Desires are achievable, but desire doesn't not have complete power to achieve them as need does". A desire can be affected and influenced by the outer and other factors.

Dream Vs Goal

Dream – As APJ Abdul Kalam sir said, Dream is not that what you get in your sleep, what that makes you not to sleep. Dream is like a wish which is considered to the higher level than want and desire. There will be many dreams in the life, but all the dreams were not fulfilled; only the important dreams may consider as achievable.

Goal – Goal is nothing but a dream, but with a plan and fixed time to achieve. When a dream is considered as important, you start a plan and decide to make with a certain plan and for a certain time period it can be considered as Goal. In a simple understanding, goals are dreams with a certain dead line to achieve them.

Goal is something which can be achieved totally by an individual; the accomplishment of goal was not influenced or distracted by any external forces.

Need Vs Desire Vs Goal

Need – *Need is totally personal to an individual. Need is the most essential, it is not effected with any external force or factors.*

Desire - *Desire and want are something different than need, it is not based on personal or individual; desire and wants are for external one and it was impacted and influenced by external force.*

Goal - *Goal is something which can be achieved totally by an individual; the accomplishment of goal was not influenced or distracted by any external forces.*

Utilize the power by Understanding

So finally considering all in a sequence:

1. The dream is to be considered first

2. Convert that dream into goal, by keeping a plan and deadline to achieve

3. Turn your goals into your needs, as the goals and needs both were totally personal of an individual and influenced by only internal force. When you feed your sub-conscious mind to get the goal as it is necessity, essential, important, and needy thing for your life, the goal can be turned as a need.

When the Goal turns into Need, it gets all the power and speed up in getting accomplished.

You have a need to breath, you have a need to eat or drink, all the needs get fulfilled by your mind no matter who you are and where you are, your needs get fulfilled; when you turn your goals into needs, they too get fulfilled by your internal sub-conscious mind and internal autonomic mind power.

> "Doing what needs to be done may not make you happy,
> But it will make you great."
>
> – George Bernard Shaw

What about your desires?

Desire is something which can be achieved in future, right? A desire is which can be achieved by number of small goals.

If you want to buy a Rolls Royce car, as it was an external force it may not be achieved easier, as it is influenced by your desire, so allow some small goals to achieve your desire.

Let's consider to get 20 Crores Rupees for getting the Rolls Royce car, the goal has power to create an income source, because the income is a necessary (needy & essential) thing for achieving the desire.

1. Goal: to get start a business
2. Goal: to make profit from business
3. Goal: to earn 20crore by 24months from this business
4. Goal: to buy a Rolls Royce with that money.

The desires can be achieved, by a group of goals. Keep goals in a way which can fulfill all your desires in your life. As you turn goals into needs, consider a chart of your desires to be fulfilled, list them and under that again list small needs which you should make in a way to achieve the big desire.

"If you don't know what you want, you'll never find it. If you don't know what you deserve, You'll always settle for less. You will wander aimlessly, uncomfortably numb in your comfort zone, wondering how life has ended up here. Life starts now, live, love, laugh and let your light shine!"

– Rob Liano

My Desire:

_____

As you turn your goal as needs it will get earlier than you ever expected. List the small needs in a sequence to achieve your big desire.

Need 1: _____

Need 2: _____

Need 3: _____

Need 4: _____

"Achieve all your big desires in your life, by making your dreams as goals, and turning your goals as your needs, by feeding your sub-conscious mind continuously. Keep small needs in a sequence, which can fulfill your BIG DESIRES".

05

Be a Dream Driven

"If you are thinking about poverty you can't get richness as If you can't get sex with your enemy"

– Dr. San Bharath

All the successful peoples were driven by their dreams. First they follow the dreams; later their dreams will drive them towards it. Dreams are the reason of becoming a masterpiece. Dreams are the fuel for success. All the successful people were successful because of their fulfilled dreams.

The man who doesn't have dreams cannot success, because successful life comes only with fulfilling his dreams. Without dreams a man cannot fulfill them and cannot become success. "If you don't have dreams to become a billionaire, you will not work to fulfill that and you can never become a billionaire in your life".

The difference between the successful or failure is only a dream. The failures really don't have dreams, though they know- if they dream and achieve them, they too can become successful. But I don't know why the failures are not dreaming and why they are not willing to live a successful lifestyle. Unlike a failure, successful peoples were followed a dream, they tried to get that dream fulfilled in their life. As they are moving towards the dream, one day the dream will become a chasing element to them and this chasing force will drive them to achieve what they dreamed.

The dream is the basement for success, without dream the building of success can just remain as a fantasy in the life. Dream with repeated thinking about a dream will become' s stronger. The stronger you make your dream, the more magical things you can see in your life with the driven force created by the dream. You can notice only the dream and the result, rest the work, the journey of making the dream everything can be happens as default with its force as a Magic.

Successful peoples do only the work what they really love to do and in what they were passionate about. Suppose if a man wants to become a billionaire, so his dream will be to become a billionaire; he does the work in accordingly what he is passionate about and he choose to do the work which he love. Such a person will learn quickly and adopt all the necessary attitudes which he need to adopt, *"man finds no difficulty in achieving their dream because he love it and he learn to get it"*. Only needy thing was keeping a dream and holding it for longer time, which majority of humans doesn't do!

Where there is a dream there is learning; where there is learning there is adopting; where there is adopting there is progressing; where there is progressing there is achieving. Here in the above process, there is no difficulty or impossibility or hard working or boredom or stress. Dreaming and achieving it is the most easiest, entertaining, enjoyable, enthusiastic and energetic thing that a man can do in his life. Without dreaming & without achieving them, life is incomplete and life will be disappointed.

"Keep a dream on a paper form your mind; Stick that paper on the wall where you see regularly, the magic happens in making a dream into reality, by writing your dream on paper"!

"If the poor were thinking regularly about his poverty,
He cannot become Rich,
For becoming rich,
The poor should change his thinking to think about becoming rich"

– Dr. San Bharath

Be Optimist for Achieving Your Dreams

If you discuss about earning a million dollar with a beggar or poor person what he can tells? If you discuss about your PhD project thesis with an illiterate person what he can tells? Do not listen to anyone who was not aware and care about your dream. You are unique and your dream is unique, so find the possible ways to fulfill your dreams; only by thinking and observing about your dreams you will get number of ways to achieve them. As the dream was arise from your mind, the way of achievement can also be found in the same mind; don't be with disbelief or conflict of thinking negatively about your dream. It is possible, put it into action. Remove the fear of failure. Un-happening make it happen you're your Action; keep doing until you do it, don't fail in doing.

Seek the positive way of making your dream into possible. Don't doubt your dream.

The Man without dream is man without Destination, the man without destination works hard but remains as failure in the life. Non-Dreamer will work with zero or minimal result.

If You Are Not Satisfied With Your Results You Are Getting, Change your Efforts & the Pathway

> *"If the poor were thinking regularly about his poverty,*
> *He cannot become Rich,*
> *For becoming rich, the poor should think to become rich"*
>
> – Dr. San Bharath

The same roads will show you the same destinations; if you want to go to Delhi you should choose Delhi road, not the kanyakumari road. If you want to go to success you should choose that and you should go on that road. Choosing the failure road and going towards failure or choosing the success road and staying there without movement cannot take you to success.

If you want to get the result what you want, change the work accordingly. All the ordinary people lost (or) ignored their commonsense in their life, so they remained as ordinary. The ordinary will work for a month and waits for the result (salary), but the masterpiece first knows the result, if he likes the result then only he does the work, if not he will choose another path, which gives the desired result which he expected.

"Becoming rich, is 100 times easier than living as poor, With compared to their daily struggling for survival of a human life"; Lack of this information the poor were remained as poor.

– Dr. San Bharath

There will be no poor or ordinary people if

"If the poor see the rich & their lifestyle through their mind's from that event he will never remain as poor again in his life". The poor is poor, because he lives with the poor and he will think like a poor and this poor thinking will make him to be limited with poorness in his life. So we see, peoples 95% born with poor and die as poor. No progress or no performance can be seen in such lives. "The reality was poor never saw the rich and the rich lifestyle and they never noticed that living in poor as hard, difficulty and peace less". But they were fighting with their lives at every moments of their life's to survive, to get proper shelter, clothing, proper health & medication etc., but they don't know the secret. "Becoming rich, is 100 times easier than living as poor, With compared to their daily struggling for survival of a human life; By lack of this information the poor were remained as poor".

Out of 100 percent, 95% who born as poor will live in poverty and die in the poverty. Only 4% of the poor will get an ordinary life, and very rarely 1% will become a rich. This is because, 95% of the people will never think about becoming rich; their thoughts were limited and influenced mostly by their circumstance, unless they come out of the regular thoughts and regular works they can't get the great results. If the poor were thinking regularly about his poverty, he cannot become Rich. For becoming rich, the poor should change his thinking to think about becoming richness.

> *"Your richness begins in your brain, And first you become rich in your brain, On the second time you will become rich is reality. Untie your brain to become rich first. It will un-tie your legs to become rich in Reality".*
>
> *– Dr. San Bharath*

The most tragedy thing of a poor man was, though the poor man born as human with all the potential and capabilities like every human brain & body; but the poor were not living a life of freedom, the poor were locked his legs and brains to move & think beyond the wall of poverty. This is most tragedy painful limitation with this social disease; it ties a man physically and mentally and remains him as a prisoner and shows the big un-escapable walls to his foresight and eyesight; this makes the poor to live with their own world within the boundaries of wall, and live in the possibility with their locks to their brains and legs.

Yet, every poor person has the platform & opportunity and all the sources to become rich and live a complete human life. But without their willing of thinking about the richness no support can change them to move even an inch. The poor were struggling to pay the EMI'S and the monthly bills, their income will be 50% less than their monthly expenses. Every day, every step, the poor will think about the next month bills and payments of interests. There will be no peaceful life to the poor, not his struggle & not his hard-work can put him out of that prison, but his continuing doing the same struggling and same hard-work, again and again, making him to remain as poor, everyday!

Your richness begins in your brain and first you become rich in your brain, on the second time you will become rich is reality. Un-tie your brain to become rich first, then it will un-tie your legs to become rich in Reality.

Solution

The poor can become Rich, not by the struggling or hard work for 20years or 30years of his life, but by thinking for 20mins-30mins about the richness every day with the UN-TIED BRAIN.

06

Desire as Passion

"Sex with no passion sucks,
Kissing with no passion sucks,
Conversations with no passion sucks,
Career with no passion sucks,
Life with no passion sucks,
A human mind can do and achieve anything;
You just have to have the passion that pushes you ahead in your life taking you a step closer to success"

– Rahul vishwakarma

You may have many dreams in your mind, but let us talk about your desire; what the desire means in actually?

Desire is not a positive Term & not a Negative Term; In fact the desire is a Force which arises in you to do something which you consider it as most necessity thing you required for your life!

Desire was an Inbuilt Force which cannot be generated by force; it only arises when want arise in you, as it INBUILT WITHIN YOU.

Desire doesn't make you feel good, it creates a pressure in you & it let make you to do such things which can fulfill that, then only the desire will disappears from you. Desire is like a Burning coal it will burn you inside to do the needy for the fulfillment of that desire, it will burn you continuously until you fulfill it; though you ignore the pain created by your Desire it doesn't stop burning you inside. It will act & burn you ever, so to relax from the burning pains the only thing you have to do with your desire is, to fulfill that immediately!

Don't let yourself to keep all kinds of desires of you at once; too many desires in you will burn you from many ways. You lose peace of mind by that pain.

"LET ALLOW YOURSELF IN KEEPING ONLY ONE DESIRE AT A TIME, WORK ACCORDINGLY TO FULFILL THEM & ATTAIN PEACE". AFTER ACHIEVING THAT, LIST THE NEXT ONE!

> *"To burn with desire and keep quiet about it is the greatest punishment we can bring on ourselves."*
>
> *– Federico García Lorca*

No End to Your Desires

There is no end to your desires; Desires last ever until your last breath, but desire changes according our knowledge, exposure, growth, time. In my schooling, I want a new cycle, in my college I want a new sports Bike, in my medicine I want a sports car, now I want National Award, success, money etc.

Can I become desire Free?

Don't waste your time too much, in thinking about your Wants & desires. Don't think about to destroy all your desires forcefully by ignoring or Masking them, the desire may Change but desire will never leave you. You can never become a desire free person; but there is an only possibility when you attain your ultimate life purpose, you may become free of all other small desires which you might already fulfill in your pathway;

So use your desire energy in helping you to get all the great things into your Life & to make you successful & reach your destination point as soon as you can!

You Are Made Through Your Desires

Desire is a force it can build you to great or can break you to the worst, it has such a power to make or break you! All the choice was in your conscious decision to be whatever!

I became A Doctor, because I want write in front of my name, this may be a small want, but that made me to learn 5years & finally made me A DOCTOR.

But later after this, I want to create a new Product which is more advanced & gives benefits to the human, this desire forced me to establish a research center for myself; it made me as an INVENTOR.

When I want to earn more money, I desire to earn more & more money, and this desire made me to start an industry & that strong desire made me a Successful INDUSTRIALIST.

I have a great stag fear as I'm more introverted person, but a want I choose to be as a leader, it made me to become a NETWORK MARKETER, leader to my huge & great team.

- ✓ My desire of becoming Rich Made Me RICH.
- ✓ My desire of becoming an Author made me AUTHOR of this Book.

All the desires I choose for myself are Progressive desires. The desire is such a force which is like a team; it can build you faster ever if you lit your Progressive desire to burn in you.

You are made through your desires, Choose your wants, accordingly how you want to be!

Get Clarity of your wants!

1. Look the possibilities
2. Look the consequences

See your benefits

   a. *Progressive Growth*

   b. *Happiness & joy*

   c. *Enjoyment & fun*

   d. *Satisfaction & Achievement.*

Look the possibilities

I want to participate in freedom struggle along with Gandhi, is this possible now? NO! Can this turns as Emergency want & burning desire for my life? NO! So here before choosing the want, I should find the possibilities & I should see the consequences in both positive & Negatives way of the Desire. So this will give me CLARITY for Choosing a RIGHT WANT & ARISE A RIGHT DESIRE.

Look the consequences

Let you may want to buy a new car; you don't have the required amount with you for buying a car, what you do? You can take a Loan & proceed to buy a new Car, you may sell your old car with minimum price or you may keep that old car with you if you don't like to sell to a low price. So here see the consequences behind your desire & Action, you should work for 3 to 5 years to pay your loan EMI's to get finance Free. If you are willing to pay for the longer duration & if you feel there is no any other financial pressure on you, then you can Proceed, if you have any other financial commitments you have to pause a while & think; then take the decision whether to proceed or to stop!

If you have a clarity that you can't or unable to get that now, you don't feel that as WANT; so, it don't turns as DESIRE to you.

"Every creation, invention happened by DESIRE of Someone"!

> *"Dreams are like living things; they can grow, they can suffer disabilities, they can have deficiency diseases and they can also die off when they meet unfavourable and favourable conditions respectively."*
>
> – Israelmore Ayivor

07

Understanding mind, knowing intention and reason!

> "Sex is the consolation you have when you can't have love"
>
> – Gabriel García Marquez

Every thought or an action projected by you from within, is not actually raised within or from the knowledge within, it's an impact, influence and materialization by intention and crafted by a reason which they believe;

Behind an every action there will be an Intention, Behind an Every Intention there will be a reason which can change the outcome of the Action; "Action is a materialized output which is Influenced and Impacted by Intention behind and Originate by a reason and beliefs in one's mind"

According to Folk psychology, "Man's every Intentional Action is a function to accomplish a Desire, Goal and Achieve some extremity which are based on the belief and which can fulfill his want and remove the pain of Desire; "THERE IS NO ACTION WITHOUT INTENTION, NO INTENTION WITHOUT A REASON". "The Action Did Without Intention Can Be Considered As A Unproductive Actions; And Action Which Do Not Carry A Strong Intention Such A Actions Will Be Considered As Useless".

Desire

Reason

Intention

Thoughts & Actions

My Action behind this book, let's consider as an example

A desire aroused in me to become an Author and public speaker by reading about Rabindranath Tagore and Swami Vivekananda.

Here the desire was aroused inside me, but it was not innately created in me; it aroused by influence of some external force – by seeing or by knowing about someone, I got inspired, that influenced & impacted myself to arise a Desire in me;

When a Desire arouse in me; my mind started thinking and crafting a reason for everything which I believe, I think about whether this desire is right or Wrong, finally I justify to myself that desire is Right mostly and I will craft reasons Why I Need To Fulfill This Desire;

The crafted reason with WHY, that became a Pillar for my intention, more over all the accepted reasons crafted by me will become my intention, and as more reason I craft with myself that much stronger my Intention will become. After the intention, the thoughts, behaviors and Attitude will arise and frames actions which all are interlinked originated from, and on the base of Intention.

As I build a Strong intention, all my thoughts, behaviors and attitude framed a great and effective Action in writing a Book.

The reason which you give to yourself will design a Quality of your intention; the Reason which you believe and agreed will create more impact on your action; A Man Framing himself with a reason can be called as Rational Person, this can be called as Rationalism!

Understand & Adopt Rationalism

Rationality is the Quality or state of Being Rational – this is, an every thought or action were agreeable to a reason; Being rational will be interlink with One's Belief with one's reason to believe and one's action with one's reason;

Reason is the capacity of consciously making sense of things by applying logic and justifying practices according to beliefs based on new or existing information in your mind. It means, if you don't have the right information & knowledge, then you may not geta right reason & judgments;

The reason may become Wrong if you are with lack of right information & incapable of your understanding Level; most of the peoples are remained as under Ordinary lifestyle because of holding not right understanding and not right information, and these NOT RIGHT BELIEFS and leading their life's to NOT RIGHT PLACE and NOT RIGHT LIFESTYLE.

Example: My Granny told my father to study well so you get good Job, you will get settled with some good salary; that salary is the purpose of your life and it's your potential;

My father understood that concept of Employment and believed that information as right, WHICH IS NOT RIGHT BELIEF, and he let his life in according to the information he accepted by him, and by seeing society doing a Job and selling themselves for salaries, So my father belief became strong it made him to create a strong reason and Moved according to his Reason;

so he got a job in a Place, which is not his actual potential & which is not the actual purpose of his life, but he stood there, which is NOT RIGHT PLACE and NOT RIGHT LIFESTYLE he is leading, it's much more less, less than 1% than his Actuality;

"YOU MAKE YOURSELF, BY WHAT YOU BELIEVE IN YOU AND WHAT REASON YOU GIVE TO YOURSELF FINALLY"

Become Selfish For Getting Your Self-Interest

"In fact, living a non interested life becomes wrong & it may lead to crime, as sex without interest become _____"

– Dr. San Bharath

If one accepts a model in which benefitting oneself is optimal, then rationality is equated with behavior that is self-interested to the point of being selfish; no one wants to be a loser, everyone on this earth wants to be a successful person, to become successful in his want, and that WANT is a relatively to become Selfish;

It's not wrong to get, what you want & to become what you are supposed to be; accept the fact, being selfish is not wrong, it's not a negative term anymore. I want my comfort and I want my success so I am selfish to become what I want, I want all my wants to be fulfilled and I am selfish to be like that. So it's actually a good & positive term everyone should adopt selfishness for living their life as they want to live in this world.

The more selfish you become, the happier you can live! The more self-less you become the more tragedy you face in your life!

Adopt Questioning & Reasoning

Meaning comes with Questioning and Success comes from Reasoning.

Questioning: *it is like a Habit which everyone can adopt in their life which can arise the meaning for their life and activities; doing a work with no Questions is meaningless!*

Reasoning: *is also like habit or intuition, is one of the ways by which thinking moves from one idea to a related idea in the mind. An interlinking with everything and every meaning raised form the Questions of your mind. The answer for every Question & solution for every problem: is reasoning, thinking & interlinking them with commonsense.*

Reasoning is the means, by which rational individuals understand sensory information from their surrounding and understand the conceptualized abstract such as the Cause and Effect of every action.

Reasoning plays an important role in increasing your ability of Self-consciousness, in terms of your decision, attitude, goals & beliefs.

> *"You have the capacity to leave a lasting impact and indelible impression upon this world...*
> *Claim the sacred spaces of your minds nurture and cultivate a vision of fulfillment,*
> *And move toward that destiny with patience, perseverance, and prayer."*
>
> – Mahershala Ali

08

Rational and Irrational Influence

"If you find no reason for a sex, you can see no pleasure in that"

– Dr. San Bharath

Humans have both innate rational and irrational leanings from the birth; innate rational leanings are self – helpful & self – constructive and the irrational leanings are which self-defeating, self-destructive;

All emotional disturbance arises within the human is because of the irrational Knowledge held with the man; knowledge with no Logics, knowledge with no values, knowledge with no reason, knowledge with no meaning, and knowledge without understanding can rise to destruction of self for no reason! Only you can make yourself destroy or disturb when your knowledge is with no reason and finds a blind view! Uncontrolled situation or an incident can never make emotional disturbance because it is uncontrolled and being uncontrolled it's reasoned!

There are no such emotional difficulties such as

Self-blame, self-pity, unwanted anger, hurting/hurt, Shame, depression, Anxiety, guilt, Addiction, Sadness, Avoidance, self-defecting, Self-destroying, emoting disturbance can disturb or destroy you, than anything else.

There will be no such destroying emotions if you are rational, because all these destructive emotions can enter only in an irrational man, who don't see or consider a reason for all!

If you make yourself to live in an unrealistic, Rigid, Illogical and unreasoned lifestyle, your mind will adopt to become an irrational mind & make you to become an irrational Man; Before everything keep a thought of WHY & HOW, you can get or understand the reason behind an everything; when you get the knowledge of Reason behind an every act, It changes your perception through a new Level & procreates your understanding to next above Level!

Beliefs about Circumstances

"Man does not get emotionally disturbed by unfortunate and unchangeable circumstances, as no one gets disturbed with a heavy rain even for continuously for 10days, but he will disturb more by waiting for10mins in the traffic";

They construct their views of these circumstances through their Understanding, their evaluative beliefs, through their acceptance level, through the education by the society and social beliefs, through the practice of number of people around in their circumstances, and through others view".

Man's Destruction in His Irrational Thoughts

According to Albert Ellis: three cores that humans tend to destroy themselves through-

1. "I absolutely MUST, under practically all conditions and at all times, perform well and win the approval of significant others. If I fail in these important—and sacred—respects, that is awful and I am a bad, incompetent, unworthy person, who will probably always fail and deserves to suffer."

   Holding this belief when faced with adversity tends to contribute to feelings of anxiety, panic, depression, despair, and worthlessness

2. Other people with whom I relate or associate, absolutely MUST, under practically all conditions and at all times, treat me nicely, considerately and fairly.

   Otherwise, it is terrible and they are rotten, bad, unworthy people who will always treat me badly and do not deserve a good life and should be severely punished for acting so abominably to me.

   Holding this belief when faced with adversity tends to contribute to feelings of anger, rage, fury, and vindictiveness.

3. The conditions under which I live absolutely MUST, at practically all times, be favorable, safe, hassle-free, and quickly and easily enjoyable, and if they are not that way it's awful and horrible and I can't bear it. I can't ever enjoy myself at all. My life is impossible and hardly worth living.

   Holding this belief when faced with adversity tends to contribute to frustration and discomfort, intolerance, self-pity, anger, depression, and to behaviors such as procrastination, avoidance, addictive behaviors and inaction.

According to REBT

The human thinking, emotion, and action are not really separate or disparate processes, but that they all significantly overlap and are rarely experienced in a pure state. Much of what we call emotion is nothing neither more nor less than a certain kind—a biased, prejudiced, or strongly evaluative kind—of thought.

But emotions and behaviors significantly influence and affect thinking, just as thinking influences emotions and behaviors. The overlap of emotions and destructive feelings were the reason for a man's destruction and under thinking; the brain is created for thinking, and just for thinking; but more over it is not used for thinking anymore.

85% peoples on the world is ready to do any kind of slavery work and labor work for their survival, they were not interested to think. Not interested to create, not interested to use their brain and to be original.

Irrational Beliefs

According to REBT THEORY, it proposes four core irrational beliefs;

1. *Demands: the tendency to demand success, fair treatment, and respect (e.g., I must be treated fairly).*

2. *Awful zing: The tendency to consider adverse events as awful or terrible (e.g., It's awful when I am disrespected).*

3. *Low Frustration Tolerance: The belief that one could not stand or tolerate adversity (e.g., I cannot stand being treated unfairly).*

4. *Depreciation: The belief that one event reflects the person as a whole (e.g., When I fail it shows that I am a complete failure).*

> *"Humans, unlike just about all the other animals on earth, create fairly sophisticated languages which not only enable them to think about their feeling, their actions, and the results they get from doing and not doing certain things, but they also are able to think about their thinking and even think about thinking about their thinking."*
>
> *– Albert Ellis*

𝓗ardness of thinking

"Thinking & understanding are the most easiest and important key elements of life, which can make you, enjoy, successful, rich and complete life"

The successful people are not handworkers; they are good thinkers.

Everyone can think, but 85% don't think. They don't show interest in thinking.

85% people remains as poor, hard worker& fools; the fool can think and underrated but don't do that; because they are fools.

They don't think for Success & Freedom Life!

– Dr. San Bharath

09

Life is by thinking

"Thinking is most enjoyable experience on world, you can't express the feel, and you just need to experience it like sex";

– Dr. San Bharath

Everything happens for a reason & by the reason; if you can think about the reason there will be no miserable Incident or unexpected results again and again in your life. Use your brain to think about the reason with WHY it happens? If not this then HOW it might be?

When you can truly understand the reason behind you can get what you want without difficulties. Life is by thinking, death is by ignorance;

Law of inter and intra relation

The world around you is equal to the world inside you; the outer world can influence & impact your inner world and your inner world can influence & impact the outer world. If the force of influence outside is higher than the strength of your thoughts it wills vigorously minion you to it. If you hold your thoughts strongly, no matter what the external force was, you can make the world to be your minion.

Let, create your thoughts first and make them stronger than the out world, project your stronger thoughts to the world, prepare yourself to the victories before the world wants to make a war with you. Don't allow the world to judge you or to declare a war with you. Create your world in your mind according to how you want to be. Hold that thought strongly until it materializes into reality.

World wants to take everything from you if you ignore or don't utilize what you have, you lose your muscle tone, if you don't make a move with your muscles for just 2 weeks. And the world wants to give everything to you what you desire more with your thoughts strongly. "A rich will become poor if he don't think about earning & becoming more rich, poor can become rich if he continuously hold his thoughts to become rich".

The thoughts are materializing elements for your life, if you think more & continuously about something to be happening and put that in action. It will definitely materialize one day and come into your real life. So you can live your life as you are thinking about you in your mind, the way you think & perceive in your mind will get act and experience with your outside world. Everything, the success, failure, sadness, richness, poverty, depression, health and wellbeing, the luxury and comfort etc. that you are seeking outside was coming from your inner mind.

A Powerful Formula for your life

What you think with a commonsense and believe that honestly with feeling, it becomes reality. You should believe what you believe strongly, and you will believe what you are decided to believe already in your mind. Remember you are more capable than what you think about you, so believe in infinity you will reach infinity. "You are with infinity power, your acceptance will make you infinity; your ignorance will make you a limited personality".

Infinity Decisions

Life gives you infinity to take the decision at every event of your life, but every decision holds its own importance; every great decision you made can lead to extent your infinity to the next level.

Infinity creations

You are created in such a way that you are a creator; you have the infinity creativity in you, by which you can achieve anything, if you believe it. Rising a human life, you are raised with infinity ideas which can create infinity creations;

Conceive your ideas; by believing in your infinity and achieve with your actions.

Infinity of habituation

You are born with flexibility and adoptability mindset; a man can live at the worst poor hut and even can live on the utmost richness; man was made of flexibility to infinity ideas & adoptability to his flexibility;

Man can habituate any kind of culture, by making his adoptability to everything he wants for his survival;

Infinity of understanding

The understanding was the highest performance which a man can do; he can achieve the highest achievements as a default with the understanding;

You are capable of understanding infinity; your brain has no limitation for understanding and acquiring the knowledge

Life Arise and Life End

Life is like an Egg, when the force and pressure from inside egg breaks the shell, it leads to raise a life of chick form the egg; If the outer force or pressure acts on the egg, the breaking of the shell from outside, leads to end the life of chick;

In the same way, the thought from your mind can give you a life; the thought is your pressure, your force, your energy and your hopes of life. Everything will raise a new life through your thinking; If the outer situation, pressure and force act on you to lead your life, it will ends you to limited; live through your ideas and thinking not through your situations and pressures;

The importance of understanding your force, whether it is developed from your inside or form outer world; make sure, your inside force should lead you always;

> *"From what we get, we can make a living; what we give, however, makes a life."*
>
> *– Arthur Ashe*

10

Developing a Rational Mindset with Epistemology

"My own sex, I hope, will excuse me, if I treat them like rational creatures, instead of flattering their fascinating graces, and viewing them as if they were in a state of perpetual childhood, unable to stand alone".

– Mary

According to Kant's, epistemology was an attempt to understand the conditions of the possibility of human understanding. Epistemology is the study of knowledge acquisition. It involves an awareness of certain aspects of reality, and it seeks to discover what is known and how it is known.

For every thought or an activity or an action you do in your Brain it was caused by the reason behind it, this reason may be unknown or known by your consciousness. But the existence of reason is there behind everything, finding a reason behind every thought & activity of your brain is called Rational Mindset.

For acquiring a Rational Mindset you should develop a knowledge which can give you noble reason and understanding the nobility way of truth & belief with justification.

> "Change will not come if we wait for some other person or some other time. We are the ones we've been waiting for. We are the change that we seek."
>
> – *Barack Obama*

For the Acquisition of rational Mindset

Epistemology study provides knowledge and distinguishes of truth, belief and Justification of every activity in a noble way. It involves an awareness of certain aspects of reality, and *it seeks to discover what is known & how it is known.*

Epistemology knowledge can be understood under Knowledge, Truth and Justification – which can give a Justified, True Reason behind everything with Right Knowledge.

✓ Knowledge

Is a familiarity, awareness, or understanding of someone or something, such as facts, skills or objects! By most accounts, knowledge can be acquired in many different ways and from many difference sources. Knowledge is among the many kinds of cognitive success that epistemology is interested in understanding.

Beyond the external knowledge, there is Self Knowledge which arises from his thinking. Self-knowledge usually refers to a person's knowledge of her own sensations, thoughts, beliefs, and other mental states.

✓ Truth

Is the property of being in accord with factor reality. In everyday language, truth is typically ascribed to things that aim to represent reality or otherwise correspond to it, such as beliefs, propositions &declarative sentences.

Truth is usually held to be the opposite of falsity. Most human activities depend upon the Truth, Most commonly; truth is viewed as the correspondence of language or thought to a mind-independent world.

Adopt a Logical Truth, believe a truth as truth when you satisfy a Reason of Logic behind the truth, which the logic should be acceptable by you, because all the truth are Logical, though you believe or not. Truth cannot be magical, even the magic also logic; Logic is concerned with the patterns in reason that can help us in telling it is true or not. Truths are concerned with, and as such there is only truth under some interpretation or truth within some logical system.

A logical truth is a statement which is true in all possible worlds or under all possible interpretations, and as contrasted to a *fact* which is only true in this world as it has historically unfolded. A proposition such as "If 2 + or x 2, then result was 4" is considered to be a logical truth because of the meaning of the symbols and words in it and not because of any fact of any particular world. They are such that they could not be untrue.

✓ Justification

Is a concept in epistemology used to describe beliefs that one has good reason for holding. Epistemologists are concerned with various epistemic features of belief, which include the ideas of knowledge & rationality.

Justification is the reason that someone holds a rationally admissible belief. Justification involves the reasons why someone holds a belief that one *should* hold based on one's current evidence. Justification is a property of beliefs is to be extended as they are held Guiltless. A justified belief is a belief that a person believes oneself to hold.

For developing a particular rational mindset in finding a right reason behind everything you should get a particular knowledge, truth and judgment in a right way, after getting complete information you can know the right reason behind.

Divinity and Reality

Dear God, My Father

Father,

"We are helpless, hopeless,

We became tired, fallen with fatigue muscles & weaken bones, fused joints, and stooped body in this society among cruel, dirty minded foxes;

Fallen on our knees, to pray you father; for hoping you to insert some good thoughts and morality for the cruel foxes and change
them into humans;

Father, we are living a fearful life; please give us strength and hope to stand up erect on both legs with courage in the heart and peace in the mind.

Father I pray to see my home earth, with no harms, my mother society without cries;

Teach us the truth, Feed us the morality, Arm us the courage, and immerse us in the honesty which can cleans all our fears and dirty thoughts;

Leave us to sleep peacefully every night". God, please grow morality in us;

Again & again till this earth exist..!

– Dr. San Bharath

Divinity of life

No 1 - Selfishness

No 2 - Jealousy

No 3 - Profitability

11

Selfishness is the Divinity of Life

> *"Be with rational egoism in Sex, and get more benefit & pleasure in that".*
>
> *– Dr. San Bharath*

It is defined as benefiting self intentionally; it is also called as rational egoism. In fact rational egoism is intentionally a good act. Rational egoism is giving importance to the self, doing everything for the self. If a man doesn't value self, can't value anyone or anything. Selfishness or rational egoism is a most necessity activity that every human should culture, it is not an evil act, and it's just a false assumption of the society as evil.

If a man is selfish to become rich, he starts an industry or company and give employment for many people's under his company. He is will work for his benefit and get profit finally. The intention is to become rich, but the consequence was creating an employment for many employees and providing the service for many customers. The more selfish a man becomes, the more higher he grows and provides more opportunities for others.

True progress and development of the world as far happen, only from the minds of people who are truly selfish in getting success in doing something.

If a man is not selfish to become success, he doesn't show interest in doing such hardness in inventing all for the society, no man works for free or selfless. "Man may work as selfless in Social service at some extent for his personal reasons, but he cannot perform like a Masterpiece for Free without selfishness"

"Intensely selfish people are always very decided as to what they wish. They do not waste their energies in considering the good of others."

– Ouida, Wanda

The most happiest, enjoyable person on the earth next to mad was only a selfish person, he does what he loves & he cares what he want to care, he is not worried about others in any manner, being selfish itself a great motivation for the human life. The most selfish can live most honesty life. Selfish is a divinity of Life, it beings a complete life.

Selfishness creates possession: You cannot create any possession if you are not selfish

When you don't get ownership by creating possession on something on this world, this world will kill you with thirst even though you are inside the water, you will be not allowed to drink the water even if you can see and touch that; the world is so dangerous, to live a human life, you need to have possession for your existence;

Possession makes you powerful and break all your impotence; possession in mind can make you rich to yourself, but the possession on the earth will introduce you as rich to the world, and it give you a power to you. You get recognition only with what you possess; this is true no philosophy can change this, unless the beggars get saluted by the public people.

All desires can get satisfied with your possession; satisfy them with what you have so you get free of wants & pressures. Joy and happiness are not possible to buy with your possession; it's not the matter buying joy and happiness when they are available for free of cost. So the possession can be utilized in fulfilling way for some more costly desires.

The possession may not make you joy or happy, But I'm sure if you are in impotence you can never get joy & happiness even in your dreams. Not the mind and not the stomach get satisfied.

> "Your conscience is the measure of the honesty of your selfishness. Listen to it carefully."
>
> – Richard Bach

There is a saying, believing of the society

"Love and relation brings happiness and liberty to human life; but possession brings suffering and destruction". This is a false statement; I think this statement might be accepted by all people who were depending on some other for his survivals; they might have no possession and no value for his life. "Because the truth was, possession brings you freedom & liberty, lack of possession makes you a slave under the one who possess. Possession doesn't bring the suffering, but the person who comes with love and relation can make you suffer".

People are living in such a dangerous world, by blinding themselves with false beliefs.

> "Your body and mind are so precious & priceless possessions take care of it and keep it peacefully"
>
> – Dr. San Bharath

Passion – Selfishness

Both the passion and selfishness come as same, in making self successful. Passion is an interest and love towards becoming something. A selfish man with passion can create miracles.

"You have to be burning with an idea, or a problem, or a wrong that you want to right. If you're not passionate enough from the start, you'll never stick it out."

– Steve Jobs

What makes the passion?

The passion is what you love to do even without profit. Think about what you can do in such a way even you don't get paid for your work. What work you can do always without motivation with your self interest. Passion can be doing something even if you need to pay something for it.

Passion gives you more pleasure in doing the work with love, more than a sex. This pleasure can help and hold's a man in making great things on this world; all the man made inventions are came from this pleasure, but most of peoples were just stopped at pleasure of sex, instead of reaching the passionate ones.

"Passion gives you more pleasure in doing the work with love, more than a sex"

– Dr. San Bharath

Selflessness

Is an benefiting someone, who may be unworthy of getting that benefit and this benefit is given to them by the term called social service; in fact this is an evil act which we are cultivated to our society, the service will make the capable person to be as a seeker in getting next free benefit; the service or selflessness is most dangerous act to the society in 2ways:

1. It makes a capable person as incapacitated.
2. Selflessness makes loosing the self, for others.

Both are dangerous events, in the first way service makes the capable person to become as incapacitated and he will be waiting for others service in getting free benefits and on the government schemes. Such a man will become a handicap to the society by hiding their potential and possibilities. The service makes a man to become mental handicap.

In the second way, the man who is making service will tune him to lose something for someone, such a man first lose interest on self, nothing is more dangerous than a man who ignores or doesn't care himself. Such an individual can do any kind of criminal activities for serving others. It may also lead to self – sacrifice;

- Though the selfish doesn't do well for the society, at least he does well for himself with his action; but the consequence of selfish actions makes good to the peoples. So it's a good act; Selfishness is the thinking, understanding, progressing with action and getting rich and better living;

- Though the selfless person is doing service to the peoples, the consequence of service harming him and the peoples of society, so the selfless is a bad act; service is collecting money from selfish earners and giving to some other; man's service makes him to become as action less!

> "Survival," I said softly. "It's selfish, and it's dark, and we've always been a species willing to do anything to satisfy our needs. Individuals have morals. Mobs have appetites."
>
> – Rachel Caine

12

Selfishness is breath of every Human

"Love is a kind of selfishness to get benefit and sex".

– Dr. San Bharath

Everyone born with Altruism nature, but people around us we see are purely selfish in their nature, this is by arising Alter Ego in them, it is like 'one needs to get others life than what they are living, this creates an ego to earn all what they don't have with them for getting what others have, so they move towards what they want, this makes them to be Selfish. Alter ego was arises for even very small things in the life, one small kid may get this by seeing someone eating an ice cream & he doesn't. An adult boy may get when he see someone having a girlfriend in their life, & he don't. A young person may get, by seeing some more money with others, than with him. "Alter ego is very good nature which can increase man's hope and possibility of infinity".

All human relationship are becoming like a sex; both the partners who participate in sex were getting personal satisfaction in satisfying their own urges & they name it as love or relationship but their inside intension was to satisfy their own urges, satisfying their own benefits in the sex, it is a kind of selfishness. "In the same way, peoples ask others to do favor for them in a relation & they called it as favors or sacrifice in relation, but their inner intension was to get personal benefit, it is a kind of selfishness.

> The Noble Truth – "Everyone on this world is selfish; but the relationship which abused emotionally wants you to not be as selfish, to sacrifice yourself for their selfishness; how unfair this world is"!
>
> – Dr. San Bharath

Some tells great stories outside to society, but inside they see their selfishness for their personal benefits. Man on this earth does no help to you without their personal benefits; if anyone is doing any help without expecting anything at that time; it means they are expecting more from them, which may be physical, psychological, professional, ethical or virtual benefits to them.

Unless you don't understand the intension and investigate the profit behind the help or service you treat it as favor or social service; but the personal benefit will be of intension, it's beyond the ordinary mind's imagination.

Once, while we are doing tree plantation in the surrounding places of my town, we planted hundreds of plants with our own money & energy, we are needed some support of men & money so we started collecting donation of rupees 10 per head, we asked hundreds of peoples, requested many times to the closed relations & friends, but we received 1200 rupees after asking 4,300peoples. No one helped for plantation because, they think plants cannot give benefits to them. I am frustrated with these selfish humans. The fact is, they didn't understand the benefit which can be happen by plantation.

It is saddest, worst situation but it's the truth that "No human will be with you, without their personal benefit". No one likes to live with a beggar; beggars will be with beggar only, because he may think in getting some help from them sometimes in his life.

Will you do friendship with a beggar? No, because you don't get any sort of benefit from him! Will you do friendship with a Doctor, lawyer, engineer, bank manager? Yes, because you will get sort of personal benefit from them. The relationship is by Selfishness & people in the relation are selfish! Don't live with the blame eyes & with the pseudo belief that "humans are good & not selfish" it is false! A woman wants a strong & huge earning men, and men wants a beautiful women with possession and intelligent as life partner, isn't this selfishness in a relationship? Where is the love & affection in the relationship?

I felt more pride & proud for getting this human life; But after knowing the truth about the people selfishness, I feel this is not pride, it is sin; getting a human life is because of our pride but living in the false is sin, the truth was world is dangerous and everyone are selfish, Accept this!

Only a tree or plant can be giver and selfless, all human are getter, acceptor, and receivers!

So pretty by seeing useless sacrifices by someone on this world because no one deserves to accept their sacrifice. "If you don't be selfish on this earth, the people will drain your blood & all the fluids from your body like a blood sucking vampires; they don't even leave the muscles & bones they breaks & smash into pieces and use them for their personal benefits". Be selfish, so you can survive, you can become rich, you can live a complete life, you can get desires fulfilled, and you can become a human.

To exists on this earth; People changed the oxygen into selfishness. If you don't accept to breathe of selfishness you cannot live happily; if not people will cheat you, even murder you with words of gun's mouth!

"If you be selfish, you will be rich & live greatly. If you are not selfish, you will be poor & you will live no more". This is the open, hidden secret of peoples in this universe.

Live your life more with yourself, don't give your time to everyone and don't spoil that or waste that. Wasting, spilling your time for someone will be losing your time, your time is limited and you are not permanent here; so be selfish to not waste your time for anyone else. Live your life for your sake, spend majority of time in your day for yourself, not for others. Be selfish, in living your time for yourself; First, understand you have only one life & limited time.

13

Jealousy and Profitability

"A real man is selfish not only in love, sex but in every aspect of his life"

– Dr. San Bharath

Never think about a man, unless you are jealousy about him and never talk with him unless you get benefit or profit by him; iam sure no one can see a beggar and feel jealousy about him, because there is nothing with him to see and feel to want from him, so jealousy will come only on who are higher and better then you, think about them and feel jealousy about them with a thought to grow better like them and better than them.

There is nothing more to think about anyone; moreover you don't have sufficient time to think about everyone instead of yourself; when you don't find jealousy about someone, don't spare time with them it's purely your time waste.

According to psychology, concept of jealousy may refer to a feeling or emotional state

Despite feeling experienced when seeing others possess objects or benefits that do not have or that we would hold exclusively, emotional state of the person who wants to possess exclusively the beloved, layout accompanied by worry and suspicion. Unlike envy, jealous "owns" a person but feels that "possession".

Possession is an essential element of life, without possession no man can live a complete human live, either he may be a monk in the forest or beggar in the roads;

The concept of jealousy

Jealousy is a sign of showing you your lacking when you observe others holding that; I am much jealous about our great Rabindranath Tagore sir, for getting such an honorable award for his writings;

The jealousy raise to a thought of becoming more and developing high; if you are not jealousy about your neighbor's new big house, you will remain in that small house ever, jealousy can leads us to develop to higher because it creates necessity. Jealousy is the root cause for all desires, dreams and goals; without jealousy man finds no interest in living as man, and he lives no more; jealousy creates hope & interest on living!

Jealousy will raise dreams, desires and goals into life, along with these it raises the signs of your stoppage at wrong place, by push you to move ahead in seeking the more comfort and beauty of life, through:

- ✓ Insecurity
- ✓ Challenge
- ✓ weakness

When you see someone for having a comfortable finance status & luxury life living, you will get jealousy about them, and it shows your financial status, and it hints your insecurities; When you don't see your insecurities, you can never raise to a secure, comfortable, and luxuries lifestyle; the immediate action of jealousy may be negative, it shows your true position, but it raises a thought in you, to become rich and live completely and greatly like others!

When you want some big, costly, more than your capability, it becomes as an obsession and challenge to you; jealousy is a strong force of human mind, it will lead you to increase your capabilities more to get what you want.

Jealousy in me by seeing a gym body, made me to build my body, even when I am too weak! I am weak, it may be my obsession but my jealousy made me to build my body.

Nothing is Free! Only nothing is fair!

Nothing is Free & Fair on this earth everything is selfish, you can understand this more deep only after you start accepting the truth "that everything Moves on Selfishness & everyone are 100% pure Selfish Peoples on this earth"!

The World is of Self Centered, all the people on the earth are living for their 'Self-Satisfaction' nothing is wrong in this, but it is un-acceptable by majority.

Will, you do job without a Salary for Life Time? Will you go to Office or Work from 9 am – 4pm work without expecting payment?

Will you donate all your Salary to Charity every month freely without expecting the good or Blessings?

Will you Get anything freely longer time, without doing work?

NO, NO, NOOO...

Everything Counts & Everything Charges, nothing is free! So expect profit from what you do!

You don't give a piece of bread to unknown, unless you want to donate that for your personal reasons! "Every fair deal or a free deal was benched with a desire behind"! All the things happened & happening on this earth was let by a Selfish Desires of Someone!

"Thoughts are just thoughts, only the selfish desire aroused in Someone's Mind made this World to be like this, and it is an unchangeable Fact". The Selfishness was not wrong, it is meaning for SELF –BENEFIT; a benefited self was desire free, an ALTRUISM action arises from BENEFITED SELF.

> *Selfishness arises from "to get self benefit" and Altruism arises from "already benefited self".*
>
> *– Dr. San Bharath*

Seek Profitability by Being Selfish and Jealousy

The man with commonsense knows the price of everything and value of nothing, this makes a man to seek whether to go with profitability or go for nothing for getting nothing;

Every aspect of life is an opportunity in getting something & making it profitable for self; if you are doing something for getting nothing then, its better don't keep doing that. Expect some profit or benefit for doing something, don't do a free service; if it is your responsibility or duty to do that, do for your duty don't be commercial at work, and if it's your social service expect something;

Expecting Profitability is not necessarily being money or any assets; it may be a relation or good will or even your satisfaction. Before doing anything, think about what you are going to get by doing that!

Profitability Calculating Mindset

Don't take risk in doing un-calculated Risk in your life, take calculated risk along with the calculation of maximum consequences of that risk. Take risk for making profit, but never do risk which is un-calculated, it may destroy you. Keep your own calculation with complete sense.

- ✓ Attract peoples for making Profitability
- ✓ Avoid loss or debit
- ✓ Spend less time laboring
- ✓ More time in leading
- ✓ Keep your own Calculation about your profit.

14

Never depend too much on others;
It means don't trust anyone Irrationally

"Love is blind, they say; sex is impervious to reason and mocks the power of all Philosophers"

– Dr. San Bharath

The secret which goes from your mouth to anyone, you will not remain in peace. So keep your secrets within you, un-necessary opening the secrets can make you loss form anyway. So don't share the secrets with trust on anyone, keep the key within you.

Any secret will remain as secret if it is only with you, when you say your secrets or mistakes to anyone, it might be a great problem to your business or even to your life. If you have a best friend and you open some secrets to him when he was your closest person, but if a un-expectancy causes a rivalry, then you have to face the problem which is related to the secret you revealed. Keep the secrets or mistakes with you only. Never slip your words for making yourself as to create an un-wanted heroism by revealing your secrets openly at any situation.

It is not about the trust or belief; it's about practical thinking of profitability. We are living in the society where most of the peoples sold themselves for the money, in the form of job-salary. It means they want money and they can able to do any work for the money, the man's intention was ready to work for 8–10hrs per day and will be working for years until he gets retired. The work of an employee was not intentionally with the love or interest towards his job, but about the necessity of money and to make money.

We are surrounded by the peoples who are selling their own self, their mind's knowledge, their educational knowledge, their time, talent & skills for money. So what cost's him to sell his values or ethics;

Coming to partners or friends in your business, everything is fine when you are with nothing but when you want to become a billionaire and move from an ordinary lifestyle, it is mandatory to maintain some distance from all the peoples who are remaining as ordinary or poor, the un-willing of people to become millionaire or billionaire will make such peoples to remain as they are. It's not a mistake to move ahead by losing them because you can't take the people who are not willing to become rich along with you.

Becoming a billionaire is like taking a new pathway, like entering into a boat from the road. If only you are willing to become a billionaire, you move alone. Never allow your ordinary or poor friends to enter in your business matter, if you are willing you can be as a friend with them but your business and your income are totally yours. Don't involve any one in them with trust or belief.

You can believe in your business

- Your upline (who will become success only by your success)
- Your Enemy (who will become success only by your failure)

You can blindly keep trust on them both, they are the only thinkers always about your success, the upline or you're the chairmen will thinks always about your success, because when you do a progressive work then only you can become success, along with you they too will become successful, so they will be always your well wisher and your supporters in your business.

You can believe your enemies too in your business, they are true; their main intention will be to overcome or to damage your business. So knowing your enemies will make you alert and progress your business and you can take all the necessity safety measures required.

> *"You can trust a man with a known intention, though if the intention is dangerous or destructive, but don't believe the one with unknown intention, go far from them"*
>
> *– Dr. San Bharath*

15

Fear is Just Your Illusion, Fear Lives until You Understand that Illusion

"An illusion what you have before sex is also a fear,"

– Dr. San Bharath

There is no any scary thing on this earth to get feared. Not the poisonous animals or a critical surgery or the deepest trench. The unknown place, an unknown language fears you, just until you know that. Once, in the beginning every swimmer will be feared of water & death, it last until they know the technique of swimming. Every fear is just until you are far from that. When you go towards it, it disappears. So fear is just an illusion.

> "In order to succeed, Your desire for success should be greater than your fear of failure".
>
> – Bill Cosby

In the same way becoming rich is also fear to the poor & ordinary people, because of this fear they will remain as they were. If you keep a step towards doing the work in becoming rich, the fear will be moving away from your way, as you move yet closer to richness, the fear disappears. "No fear can hurt or stop you; only you will stop yourself with the fear of unseen or unknown". Don't fear to fear of anything; because every fear is just an illusion, there is no scary thing on this earth.

Understand your fear; it is just an illusion because it has no power to stop you!

> "Your richness begins in your brain and first you become rich in your brain, on the second time you will become rich is reality. Untie your brain from the fear of thinking about becoming rich, when the brain preaches the richness without fear, it will make you rich in the reality".
>
> – Dr. San Bharath

You Have a Great Brain to Protect You

The purpose of your brain is to think, not to worry or fear or feel depress or something else; you got this brain in a way to get "what you are suppose to be & to make you succeed without fear";

> "Everything you want is on the other side is fear"
>
> – Jack canfield

97% people on the earth are living in the dreams, they are not about to ought their dreams to turn them into reality; 97% people believed that, they don't have a super brain in achieving a great accomplishments for their life.

"This is because of limitations they created in them; in reality, they are a limitless possibility limited with their own limitations which are truly logic less & meaningless".

These 4 Mistakes made by 97% people, which made them to remain as ordinary & poor man category:

1. *Fear of something*
2. *Under-Estimating Their Brains*
3. *Ignoring Their Will*
4. *Cynical To Their Possibilities*

"Fear makes you stop to Unknown, Fear pulls you back, it stops your progress; fear drags you to adversity life. Just think why you are feared? You get no right Answer"!

– Dr. San Bharath

16

A Reason of Surrender

"Every man knows a reason to surrender for sex, employment, majority don't find reason to surrender to their dreams and richness"

– Dr. San Bharath

All Skills and knowledge & the Art are learnable, there is nothing like which cannot be learned & even Un-Learned on this earth;

A Physical trainer working in a gym, he says- "We make any person to mould into a new shape with 90 days Workout".

When a new customer comes for weight reduction, this trainer started asking them this Question: "Sir this is 90 days concept for weight loss program and body reshape and asks to customer whether he believes in this concept or not"; Based on their YES or NO he divided into 2 groups.

If customer says YES, the trainer tells the customers to come & do exercise for 2Hrs in the morning, and If customer says NO, the Trainer tells the customer to come & do exercise for 2Hrs in the morning & 2Hrs in the evening also; finally by the end of 3months both group customers got approximately nearby equal fitness.

Here the result was based on the belief; if you believe and work, you need to invest less effort; if you don't believe and work you need to invest more effort. And the result is same for both, but time consumption is more.

Anything can be learnable & re-learnable but the thing differentiating was whether you want to keep more or less effort, based on your belief and acceptance. If there is an art or skill which you want to learn, first accept with all your consciousness keep a belief on you so you can learn easily. If you don't have belief then also you can learn that, but it needs more repetitions form you.

> "Man cannot discover new oceans
> Unless he has the courage to lose sight of the shore"
>
> – Andre Gide

Be ready accept the change with your willing, the life is not of being restricted and stricken in some situation which making you to feel in the comfort, seek for the real comfort. Don't stop at a zone with your compromise and limitations! It's not your true comfort zone; don't let yourself to die there!

Your reality is the reflection of your strongest belief; what you believe strongly, you will become that. If you see something regularly believe it, you will become that.

Have a conscious thinking, if Ratan Tata can become a most successful industrialist, if Ambani can become a most successful business man, If P.M Narendra Modi sir can become a most successful leader, and you can also become a great personality like them. Becoming something better than you, and get more comfort than today; imagine an utmost great possibility about you and see yourself there, and believe it. "Just believe in you and move ahead to where you want & what you want to become. If you believe you can get better comfort than today, you can get better comfort", Keep moving don't stop and die there!

> "Comfort is your biggest trap and
> Coming out of comfort zone your biggest challenge."
>
> – Manoj Arora

Concept of Comfort Zone

"Finding a comfort zone is not wrong, and it is right! But stopping there is wrong". The comfort zone is of 2 types:

- ✓ True or real comfort zone (your life destination point)
- ✓ False or fake comfort zone (your life destructive point)

Generally everyone think that comfort zone is about the false comfort zone, so our perception about comfort zone is purely negative. "But the actual meaning of comfort zone is most powerful zone where you are given with all kinds of magical powers, you are the man with all the possibility in your life, there is nothing impossibility for you; such a zone is your true comfort zone".

"The comfort zone where you are powerful, and the power will progress and increase day by day is your true comfort zone". "The comfort zone where you imagine that you are powerful but you are not, it is your false or fake comfort zone".

The purpose of life is to live a comfortable life by getting all desires fulfilled. so we create a comfortable place, comfortable work & comfortable situations but the misconception with the comfort zone was, choosing an false comfort zone as comfort zone and remaining there by faking yourself. This faking yourself was making you to live at very low and small with your life, not even 1–2% of your possibility.

So many people tell that comfort zone is wrong and destructive for you. But actually, in reaching the false comfort zone majority of people limit them. Choose the Right comfort zone for your life, where you must be achieved all your Dreams, Goals, desires, happiness, joy, possession and the life which you want to live. Such a place will become your actual comfort zone.

Egg shell is the false comfort zone for the chick, it feels the shell as more safety zone so it tries to remain, but the life begins only when it comes out of its zone;

A true comfort zone for your life is where you are supposed to be, with achieving the maximum possibility in this life.
A false comfort zone can be found is all the way of your journey to stop you and to kill you there itself.

– Dr. San Bharath

If your dream and goal is to become a Billionaire and successful person, but you are struck with your job salary and if you are enjoying that life, it is not your comfort zone it is fake zone. You can't live happily unless you satisfy your dream hunger. Be as a hunger, being honest with yourself about what you want. Yes, it is true you don't get satisfied with your un-filled dreams & un-filled desires, be unhappy with truth, don't be happy with fake zone.

"A true comfort zone for your life is the ultimate destination of your life, But a false comfort zone was destructive of your life".

– Dr. San Bharath

I am never a satisfied person as I know me, because many strives are running in me & they were burning me to take me home of my comfort; but my True comfort zone or home is too far, as my dream list & goals list are too long. I am sure unless all my dreams, goals & desires were fulfilled I can never be satisfied. I want to be honest with myself, I am not a satisfied person; I don't allow me to fake myself, even if I am burning & dying with the unsatisfied hunger.

"Don't false your hunger, achieve them in reality"!

Will you be honest with yourself?

> *"We have to be honest about what we want and take risks,
> Rather than lie to ourselves and make excuse to stay in our comfort zone".*
>
> – Roy T. Bennett

Life Is Like a Treasure Finder

A FALSE COMFORT ZONE is beautiful place, but nothing can possible there, because you are powerless there.

A TRUE COMFORT ZONE is very beautiful, most powerful, and magic happens there; nothing can impossible there. When you feel the sense of magical things happening in your life and when you are able to make all the impossible into possibility, then that can be called as your TRUE COMFORT ZONE OR YOUR MAGICAL ZONE.

Life's purpose is to reach the home of your comfort zone; in the way of reaching your home, you get all the distractions, false perceptions, mirages and pleasures in between. The goal of everything is to stop you with many kinds of traps in reaching your home (True comfort Zone).

All these distractions are there to distract & stop you at wrong zone; life shows you the money, for distracting you and to limit you in an office which is at corner of your city. Life shows you a way of addiction for happiness, in the form of alcohol, drugs, sex etc., though they are a just a part of your life, but they try to conquer your life. Life shows you un-wanted emotions & relations to lock you with unseen chains in a home. All these and many other trails can try to stop you, in reaching your dreams, in fulfilling your goals in satisfying your wants and in making yourself an extreme possibility and a billionaire.

So let be a treasure finder of your life with all your sense of understanding and with the brain you are given by; think.

Divinity and Reality

The comfort zone, in which you are here in the above figure, is you're false or fake zone and the zone which you are supposed to go is your true & magical zone to your life.

"Do one thing every day that scares you."

— Eleanor Roosevelt

17

Time is Irreversible Gift

"The best time of day for the sex is anytime because it is sex"

– Cameron Diaz

I don't want to consume your time in discussing more management techniques about time; in fact there is no need to have such management techniques for you, when you understand:

- ✓ The time is irreversible,
- ✓ Time is limited
- ✓ There is no good or bad time
- ✓ Once wasted time can never come backs, even you cry;

Man's time is priceless than the animal time, because our time is not just to be happy or joy, but it is to be useable;

"Don't watch the watch, keep doing"

– Dr. San Bharath

The time should be

- ✓ Used for profitable way,
- ✓ To enjoy the excitement,
- ✓ To destroy something or self.

The time is considered as used, when it can be used for making a progressive steps and profitable way of life, by thinking and working regarding your purpose and desire oriented.

The time is considered as used, when you are enjoying the present movement, no matter what work you are doing and how hard, if you're enjoying it, it is considered as utilized.

Even destructing something or even yourself can also be considered as utilized, because you are not passing the time or wasting your time, you are doing something; the act considered secondary but the primary act was you are doing something.

> *"When you find nothing to do with time, when you are boredom and passing your time to shore, it's the best moment to do sex and enjoy the time instead of spilling at shore"*
>
> *– Dr. San Bharath*

Time Push you back in your life

The only thing a Man cannot control the most valuable thing in his life was the Physical Time; the time is limited for everyone 24hrs/day, no one can escape from this not the Rich & not the thief, not the scientist & not the terrorist; every human has limited time to live their life this is acceptable fact;

The thing is whether you are utilizing the time or wasting by ignoring that, the time never pauses for anyone. Most of the peoples whom I saw around don't respect & recognize this fact, that they too have very limited time in their life to leave, but they will be losing that time by Time killing & time passing events.

How to utilize TIME

Doing something can be called as utilizing the time; whether you can enjoy the time or do any progressive work or even a destructive work can also be called as time Utilization;

Doing nothing, just passing the time is insulting the time & insulting your life itself. The one who does nothing & keep most of this day Quite in passing the time with boredom, can remain as mostly at very low level of human life, Low level in the sense of mental ability, physical capability and financial aspect as Poverty;

Because though you do nothing according the time, you will be pushed down by one step every day; as time is moving ahead and if you are just passing with doing nothing in your life will make you remain their itself, being their itself is becoming low and moving down by day by day; because time never stops moving ahead.

Let's see an example

My friend Dumchick: Borrowed 50Lakhs rupees for interest of 2Rs (24%) from his cousin sister for maintaining his transportation business, but uncertainty happened to his business some disturbance among the partners & this misunderstanding made his income stopped suddenly; he got an offer to take all his investment back from the company or to continue in that even without profit until the settlement with other partners; he chosen to continue with the business without profit for a while, but another uncertainty happen, suddenly the demand or season of business was down, but he and other partners should arrange the money from the outside for the maintenance of the business;

He is doing nothing, just passing the time by waiting for the profit or payment back from the partners. 6months happened without noticing; yet he is doing nothing, just waiting or passing the time without his activity or action. It passed 10 months without paying the interest or the principle amount; on 12th month, Dumchick's cousin sister came to him and asked about the interest & principle amount by showing the calculated list with total amount-

I calculated interest for the principle amount and also interest for un-paid interest. So this is the calculation below:

Total Principle amount: 50,00,000/-

The calculation interest with principle amount was total = Rs: 63, 41,205/-.

As he killed his time or passed the time of 1year, but he was pushed down with a due of Rupees 13,41,205/- as interest for his principle amount; if he does nothing & pass the time for two or 3 more years what will happen, he has to pay double the amount of principle amount; the time makes you backward, if you don't move along with time you remain as failure or loser;

The real competitions & real challenge for all the humans is not the human's, their own limited time & the nature (their own surrounding circumstance). You are ought to understand your competition was not with a man, but with your ever moving & limited time.

The waste time can be considered as Dead

Don't neglect and ignore the time in spending with friends for chit-chat, for an entertainment, by time passing for simply sitting etc.

> "Clocks slay time... time is dead as long as it is being clicked off by little wheels; only when the clock stops does time come to life."
>
> — William Faulkner

God has given a limited time for you, god will be observing everything about what you are doing by the given time, God allotted Chitragupta for writing about your time, he will write all the utilized time as time used, and the rest of the time which was wasted, passed, slept etc., considered as dead; by that you life will be calculated, how many hours you are alive today? And how many hours you are dead today.

> "Time is not the main thing, it's the only thing"
>
> — Miles Davis

No man is can live the whole 24hrs a day, the max you conquer your day to live the maximum you can conquer in your life. The max you can get, from your life. Try to live & utilize your time at least 10hours per day; practice this continuously and live effectively, by using more time day by day.

> If time be of all things the most precious, wasting time must be the greatest prodigality.
>
> — Benjamin Franklin

Time is limited: no extension

A rich businessman on his death bed crying with the cancer pain, and that was a last day for his life; He called doctor and requested him to extend his life 2 more days by taking all his possession of 2billions dollars for giving 2 days. Doctor said it is not possible sir; later doctor came and asked him, what you want to do if you get time of 2 days sir?

He replied, "I will finish my writing work"!

Time killer

> *"Your time is way too valuable to be wasting on people that can't accept who you are."*
>
> *– Turcois Ominek*

Don't allow everyone to come and walk in your life, they keep their foot prints in your mind and leaves you one day. But their prints will be disturbing you always and killing your time repeatedly. It's not their mistake, it's totally yours, allowing everyone into your mind is your mistake.

Never allow any man in your mind, Un-less you are jealous or profitable by them.

> *"There's never enough time to do the entire nothing you want."*
>
> *– Bill Watterson*

Disease, Disorder, Disability & Death

> *"If you want to conquer the anxiety of life, live in the moment, live in the breath."*
>
> *– Amit Ray*

They are certain; no man can escape from all these. Live your life before you leave this earth.

- The disease makes you week, so your usage of time will become low;
- The disorder make you disturb, so your usage of time will become disturb or irregular;
- The disability makes you incapable, so your usage of time reduces too down;
- The death, you have no more time to use, you are out of time.

All these are certain, take care of your health and protect yourself, live each and every movement of with fullness;

> *"In the end, just three things matter: How well we have lived, How well we have loved, How well we have learned to let go"*
>
> *– Jack Kornfield*

18

Live in Recluse
At least 30 min a day

> "Sex is excitement, seeks satisfaction and soon loses interest - selfishness. Making love is passionate, fulfilling and does not look for an end – selflessness".
>
> – Barry Long

Solitude is the state or situation of being alone; recluse is the next level to an attained solitude. A recluse is a person who lives in voluntary seclusion from the public and society.

There is no need to be a monk and go to the mountains by selling your possession to find solitude and enjoy the recluse. Solitude is ultra-connectedness with the self. There is no influence of the place or the position a man exists. It's just a pseudo belief that everyone assumptions were, under a tree or in the forest area only can makes them a Recluse.

> "I never found the companion that was as companionable as solitude. We are for the most part more lonely when we go abroad among men than when we stay in our chambers."
>
> – Henry David Thoreau

Recluse is the most needy and important that you have to attain as a Habit for yourself. This is for a reason: it's only when we are alone that we can reach into ourselves and find truth, purpose, beauty, soul, meaning, and way to life. Some of the most famous successful peoples have a great conversation to their deepest knowledge through being a Recluse, they treat this is the habit which unfold them to infinity.

> "Let me tell you this: if you meet a loner, no matter what they tell you, it's not because they enjoy solitude. It's because they have tried to blend into the world before, and people continue to disappoint them."
>
> – Jodi Picoult

Why to be Recluse & spend 30min in solitude

> "I care for myself. The more solitary, the more friendless, the more unsustained I am, the more I will respect myself."
>
> – Charlotte Bronte

1. Time for thinking
2. Time for creating a space for yourself
3. To get Deeper knowledge about you
4. For guidance from your deepest mind (SCM)
5. For communicating with SCM
6. For understanding & unfolding knowledge
7. For being peaceful
8. To be alone

How to get Solitude

"The more powerful and original a mind, the more it will incline towards the religion of solitude."

– Aldous Huxley

First get disconnected to the world which you are living, where ever you are; you get disconnect from the technology like mobile, internet and social networking.

Get alone; see a comfortable place where you can get silence without disturbance. Sit in silence not in meditation, and do nothing and welcome all the thoughts you can get; then you will get thinking about you and go deeper thinking about yourself. Accept the calling from your deeper mind; only solitude can be with you ever, not the family and not the friends, so give priority to yourself at least once a day.

"I live in that solitude which is painful in youth, but delicious in the years of maturity."

– Albert Einstein

Find time & space each day to be solitude, for improving your mental health, this is the time which you are investing for your mental health & mental strength development. This time will pay off for you in the long run. You will become a sensible person with the ability to care about your life, it progress you to the next level than your yesterday; on a chronic practice you will get to learn to be with joy & fun with you. So it is more important to create the time from your busy schedule, instead you can sacrifice your entertainments like TV, chatting, some news or social network. Learn to spend time regularly, in the beginning it may be difficult to do, but later you enjoy being as recluse.

> "Solitude gives birth to the original in us, to beauty unfamiliar and perilous - to poetry. But also, it gives birth to the opposite: to the perverse, the illicit, and the absurd."
>
> *— Thomas Mann*

As most of the peoples are getting trapped with the technology and in the struggle of earning, they are losing themselves from their life. They are losing the most important & essential aspect in their life. Life without solitude will be just like, moving with an unknown to unknown and for unknown.

> "How much better is silence; the coffee cup, the table. How much better to sit by myself like the solitary sea-bird that opens its wings on the stake. Let me sit here forever with bare things, this coffee cup, this knife, this fork, things in them, myself being myself."
>
> *— Virginia Woolf*

19

Break the emotion which Breaks you

Don't be control in sex, be control in your emotions!
Sex is good than emotional disturbance.

– Dr. San Bharath

A girl took 9 months of care, love and responsibility from her mother to born as human being. Though reaching such great life she again had born as worst animal to her emotions which caused by her situations. She involved herself to live according to her intense situational emotions instead understanding the noble truth and the reason, every time she will be coming as a new animal from her emotions. As a crying, or shouting or hurting animal; this animal makes her to lose happiness & peace in her life and others; it even makes herself in losing self.

"A man without control over his emotions and feelings is no more a man, he is an animal".

– Dr. San Bharath

Let don't be dragged by your situation, and let don't be pushed by your emotions and feelings, which are temporary. You should know where & why to move with all your sense & act according to it. Don't ever dare to spoil the noble truth & don't mislead your way by involving unnecessary feeling in your acts and belief.

If any person or a situation was the reason to the cause an emotional disturbance in you, just move out of the situation & that person's life. Don't worry about the loosing such relations & situations, they doesn't deserve to be any more in your life. Have a dare to move out of the place & person which disturbs you emotionally, if you ignore & give the second chance to them, then that mistake is yours. There will be no second chance for life & there is no Second chance.

"Your emotions and feelings will definitely change your belief & deceive you away from the truth". So don't believe the emotions & feelings, if you want to do some act just find the answers to these questions:

- ✓ What you want to do?
- ✓ Why you want to do?
- ✓ How you are going to do?

When an emotion enters in your life, you are allowed to sacrifice not just the money, but more & unfair things.

Emotions are 2 types:

- ✓ Conditional Emotions: Human emotions (Breaks you).
- ✓ Unconditional emotions: Animal, Nature, material & non-material emotions (Makes you).

Human emotions – Love, care, fear, anger, sadness, disgust, trust etc,.

May be emotions & feelings were introducers of the word – Sacrifice, Selfless, self denying & self killing – suicide etc; The HUMAN EMOTIONS were very sensitive, as the man look them as sensitive. If you ignore them, the impact & force of emotion will be less, but no man dares to ignore & neglect it; At least you do my dear reader!

Man is such a person, who has energy & he can access all the energy form the universe, and he charged that energy to his emotions too, so they got energy; but the energy of emotions were becoming day by day like an evil energy which are destroying human who gave energy & concern them.

Human Emotion can make you to kill all your desires, dreams & the purpose of your life by your own hands, makes you to be as a self denying human; Emotions can make you to kill your self – suicide". All such dangerous acts can be played by the Human emotions. If you involve & allow yourself in the world of emotions, it means you are allowed to live between powerful guns and missiles which can destroy you into pieces.

The human emotions are mostly unfair; Don't concern & consider the human relations, they are just like deals of buying & selling. If someone is sick, they take your money, take your time, take your presence with them & keep you like a slave & to serve them; they call this as Love, caring, relationship etc. But it is their selfishness & yours foolishness sacrifice. You will sacrifice all your money, energy, time &self respect;

Selfless – you will lose yourself for others, you lose self; it is self denying, you will lose your dreams, desires, goals finally you will lose your identity;

Self killing – emotion kills you from your inside when it enters in you. It makes you to kill your 'self' by separating you from your 'self'.

A relational emotions, human Emotions can make you cry, laugh, struggle, stress, anger, jealous etc,. That makes you to struggle, that makes you feel sad, cry, that makes you to get anger & destroy yourself by or for them, that shows you all the hell in your life while you still alive. "Burning your death body among the fired woods is very best than burning your 'self' everyday by being among the human emotional relations on this earth".

Don't lose your identity & originality by relational emotions, which never keep you happy, it always sit on your head as a burden, by this burden you will neglect your life, great achievements, your potential and your purpose; you remain as ordinary!

If you want to live your life happy & peacefully

- ✓ "Break all your human relational emotions in which you are involved".

(Or)

- ✓ "Convert the relational emotions into rational emotions".

I still find many people around us though they know the meaning, definition, explanation & more about the human Emotions how they are harming & destroying them, still they don't accept themselves; so pretty about such people.

2 types of peoples I can see in related to this human emotions:

1. Who accept the truth & don't sacrifice self for the human emotion. They do the fair deal, loose less for small, more to big & don't lose complete self for anything else on this world; live as selfish people; In fact they are intelligent – realize the practical life.

2. Who don't see the noble truth & don't understand their sacrifices & loses, will be living with a masked vision of emotions & lose the self; live as self less people they don't see the practical & real life.

If you want to live your lives happily & meaningfully 'break all your human emotional relations in which you are involved'.

– Dr. San Bharath

You will identify the real image of you, only when come out of all the human emotional relation net. Until you be in that net you were immersed with some pleasures & more pressures, your thoughts & mind will be in balancing these pleasure & pressure, this can take a life time period; so many peoples who are born to reach great & do great for the nation & nature but they doesn't reach their potential even 1–2% of their capability & potential. "You will earn greatness, money, pleasure, happy & peace of mind; when you don't involve in human relational emotions. You deserve to live as a selfish in this universe; don't sacrifice your–self for the human relational emotions".

If you don't be as a selfish, then you have to burn, sacrifice & die your "self" everyday with the fire called Human relational emotions. It makes you to feel anger, though you need not to react; it makes you to cry, though you need not to lose sense; it makes you to lose peace, though you need not to lose yourself; it makes you to kill yourself, though you hold strong hope on your will.

"How you find time, energy, enthusiasm, excitement, joy & peace of mind to do a new work where you find to unfold your potential & earn more happiness, more energy, more money, more enthusiasm, more excitement, more joy & more peace of mind. When you earn all these you will become RICH. To become RICH, break all human emotions around you, in which you are dying every day."

You can't become a masterpiece if you can't control or convert the relational emotions to rational emotions.

20

Break the Hurts and Sufferings

> "Love Hurts, but sex not".
>
> – Dr. San Bharath

Understand the nobility behind everything and every situation which you see in your life being Neutral. When you see some situation with your feelings and emotions you will find it as favor or Unflavored according to your feeling or mood at that situation, and you cannot see the noble truth.

Human was differentiated apart from all the living kind in nature by their understanding capacity & understanding nature, if the one who cannot understand any situation or incidents around him or her, it is their curse.

So if you find yourself sometimes unable to understand something, just get alone and keep calm & relax. After relaxation just split the situations into some small compounds and then see it in a simple manner for better understanding. If you see anyone talking or doing thing without proper understanding, just leave it off and go away; don't ever dare to make that person to understand with Arguments.

Un-understanding hurts you and others, it creates pain to you and to all. You need more knowledge to improve your understanding status. Spend with you, you will see deeper level in you & you will know your strength and weakness.

Your understanding can help you in removing all your Guilt; the knowledge which you earned by understanding & observation can help you in coming out of all your sin. The Guiltiness in your mind can never keep you calm & happy. You have to remove all your Guiltiness from your mind & thoughts; feeling Guilty may caused by any acts or thoughts which go against you, so don't ever accept the acts or thoughts which you don't see as correct to you.

Hurting is the cause of all the sufferings; accepting the hurting too deeper will leads to trap in suffering; ignore the hurt at its basic level.

Understand the concept of hurting

Hurt happens by weak people. Hurting someone is Curse; Hurting by someone is your mistake; Hurting your self is Sin. No one has right to hurt anyone in this nature.

If you hurt others, it means you are weak & you need to develop the strength. Only weak peoples can hurt others, by their words or actions or by emotions. If you don't have capacity & courage to reach someone's success or happiness, you will get anger on them which can be shown to them in the way of HURT.

If others hurt you, it means you are weak. If you are weak, you will allow yourself to react with every small useless incidents or situations; so people & all will hurts you.

If you hurt yourself, it means you are fool. Only the peoples who are with abnormal mindset can hurt themselves, if you hurt yourself anytime remember your mental situation was not proper, you need a Doctor to see your condition.

Just remember only the mad & weak peoples will hurt self & others. Don't be as a reason in hurting others, don't find the others as a reason to your hurt, & don't find false explanations to yourself. "You are strong, you are born as strong & you are going to lead your life very strongly without any hurts to others, by others, by self!"

Don't giving chance to hurt you, in any condition or human. Be strong & dare every situation with your strong mindset. Don't hang to the emotional situations they not just hurts you, even kills you.

"Understand the concept of hurt, and find yourself to be free of all hurts & so you get space to earn Richness."

If you find any relation hurting you, just break that relation and move on. You should accept to break your relation with them to be free of hurts by such peoples who are incapable in understanding.

The poison in cobra snake is not to kill others, but it is to be protected from all other poisonous on the world. "The more poisonous & dangerous person on the world was who have controlled emotions, with understanding & rational thinking"

No force can disturb or destroy this poisonous man; he can live his life with no distraction!

> "The dangerous person is who can observe and understand, the strongest person is who can think, and poisonous person is who can control his emotions by understanding & thinking". Generate venom in you, be a poisonous person; if you are poisonous no other poison can kill you, before any venom shows on you develop venom in you!
>
> – Dr. San Bharath

Suffering Creates in your Mind

As how your body creates waste secretion, excretions & toxic substances from the body; in the same way your own mind creates suffering to you. Suffering is a feeling, which disturbs continuously and drags you away from the peace & happiness.

How mind creates suffering? "With all your Acquired knowledge & unripe thoughts"

Concept – An idle human or animal don't acquire any suffering in their minds, because the suffering was created only by the knowledge & the development which you acquired in this universe.

Be aware of your thoughts!

Your thoughts are formed by your experiences; as you get more experience, thoughts changes as wiser. How wise thoughts you get that much wise you become. As you give energy to our thoughts, it will bring meaning to your experiences. The unfulfilled thoughts of your mind lead to suffering. If any thoughts arise in you, you should give energy and fulfill them with all your knowledge & intelligence; change your relationship of thoughts & mind, mind is like a tree, and it produces seeds like thoughts; all the seeds should fall on the ground and they should give rise to an individual plants, so the trees life become meaningful if not the seeds will become burden to the tree; every thought arise in your mind should become free and become fulfill, if not it will become burden to your mind & creates suffering to your mind.

To be free & peace minded person, you should have no thoughts arise from your mind; if once the thought was arise from your mind, it have to fulfill, if not you will suffer. Get control over your mind first and stop generating unwanted thoughts, if you don't control your mind's thoughts your mind will get control over you and makes you as servant to it.

Solutions to stop or remove the suffering in your mind

Answer is a single word – "Self awareness"

Remember "All solutions are hidden in self awareness; getting self awareness is observing self".

The noble truth, there is no one on this earth to guide you, judge you, correct you & remove your suffering in all the moments of your life. Only you are the person to do this, for yourself; this can be done by self awareness. Get aware of your own self instead of knowing other useless things to you. Don't show interest on knowing others, because no one wastes their time & interest on knowing about you in this busy moving world.

It became very mandatory to know about all your acts, thoughts, and knowledge; all the men's loosing self in this technological world, and wandering like blind peoples in a dark night, on the irregular roads in finding their own selves; But the men don't finds his self in anywhere on this earth, because he lost his self within him, he finds within through self awareness! Only self awareness is the way to find the self; no other way, no other place, no other work can help you & anybody in finding their own selves! "The man is differentiated with all other living kind with having self awareness; the man who doesn't have self awareness is not called a man".

Can you imagine a men moving without head on his neck; there will be no vision from his eyes, no hearing ears, no speech & taste from his tongue, no thoughts from his mind, no proper senses; man will be like this with loss of his commonsense, man will be living exactly like this who loss his self due to lack of self awareness; but man don't understand this about his or her living like a lifeless body because he have lost his sense of understanding too. The one who is living with self awareness only living like a human, and all other are just living.

21

Self Made Man

"When young be aware of fighting; when strong be aware of sex; when old be aware of possession".

– Confucius

The secret of self made man was, his habit of always doing what make him to move in a progressive and developing manner for attaining the utmost possibility he can become. The habit can become stronger as you do repeatedly, when you practice a progressive habit, you will never remain as same again & again.

"We are what we repeatedly do. Excellence, then, is not an act, but a Habit".

– Aristotle

You are what you repeatedly do; you are the result of all the habits you had tilled yesterday. You are here because of you, what you are now and what you are in your future is because of you & your habit. You cannot change the past, but you can change your future by changing your present habits. Habits can be changed & can be learned and also can be un-learned.

You can make a new decision about new habits to be learned and to change some bad habits turn to good and you can also unlearn the habits, which can't be changeable. This is possible, by your determination and your decision; when you know, you are the result of your habits, for getting the result what you want, and you need to change your habits according to that. So your habits were based on your desired results. Decide what you want, your habits will change according to them.

There is no limitation for yourself, not the circumstance and not the obstacles, but you're thought! If you think you can, you are right – you can; if you think you cannot, you are right – you can't. Decide yourself what you want to be & how you want to be.

"First forget inspiration, habit is more dependable. Habit will sustain you whether you're inspired or not".

– Octavia Butleraren

Motivation is what gets you started. Habit is what keeps you going. The inspiration or motivation cannot make you successful, they can just raise a thought to create a new habit in you, and repeated habit can make you repeatedly and one day it makes you are what you tried to become. If you seek always for the inspiration or motivation, you are no more going to become successful. Seek a habit from the motivation, not the motivation!

Most of the successful peoples are successful because of their successful habits, and most of the un-successful peoples are un-successful because of their un-successful habits. You are totally made of your habit, you habit is totally made of your intention and your intention is totally made of your thought. If you have a thought of becoming a millionaire, you will do and act with intention of becoming a millionaire, and this intentional activities repeatedly doing will become a habit, and this habit repeatedly doing will make you millionaire one day.

"I fear not the man who has practiced 10,000 kicks, but I do fear the man who has practiced one kick 10,000 times".

– Bruce Lee

The more you repeat, the more perfect & expect you become in that, the more expert you become, the more excellence you can perform, the more excellence you perform the effective result you can get. The person with a habit can make his works and task many times quicker & many times perfect than the man with no practice or habit.

> *"You will never change your life until you change something you do daily. The secret of your success is found in your daily Routine".*
>
> *– John c Maxwell*

Habit Makes You Success

Why only few peoples are more successful, while many are living an ordinary or failure life?

Success– I define success as the way you want to live, in achieving all the accomplishments, all your desires, goals and dreams in your life by learning & developing your capabilities and by adopting good progressive habits, which can make you ever successful by your habits.

Every human desire to become a Millionaire in their life: because by reaching a millionaire lifestyle, they will see the real comfort in their life, who doesn't what to life a comfortable life?

When you see the success or result, the work will become your addiction, the problem with most of the failure is, they cannot able to see the result of their work, and they can just able to see their work. The advantage of successful peoples is, they can able to see the result of their work before they start and they start for their result. When you can able to see the result very beautifully, there is no motivation or inspiration is needed for making you to work, you will be addicted for that; like an alcoholic adductor, no addicted drunker likes the taste of their drink but they just drink for the final result of Kick.

The mind of human is in such a way, it has all the driving force which can take you to all the desired result, but the thing here is, whether you are desired to go at that particular result or not, just thinking cannot make you addicted to drive yourself to the desired result, you need to desire for it and think repeatedly and imagine yourself at that result, when you see your success or result, your work will become as your addiction.

> "Successful peoples aren't born that way. They become successful,
> By establishing the habit of doing things unsuccessful peoples
> don't like to do".
>
> – William Makepeace Thackeray

Habit of Failure and Never Give-Up

Failure is not a bad thing or a negative thing, failure is the stepping stone of success, a combined group of failures are the steps of success;

Unexpectedly I got a thought to try an invention regarding a dynamo and motor related work, I am very much new to this field as my background was medical I am unknown to the entire mechanism of these, but I wanted to finish the work, I bought a motor, dynamo, battery and some related circuit board and other necessary materials. I tried to connect them in all the way which I want to make, the concept what I am thinking was clear to make so, but it was not happening in practical, I tried again and again – I failed again and again. In the process of failing many times, I learned how the motor, dynamo and batteries work; I understood the mechanism of their working.

I wanted to take help form some other who are experts in this, I meet a physics professor of a university and I explained my concept to him, he wondered by listening my thought. He called 3 of his PhD students and explained my thought to them and allowed them to work on my concept as their project of their PhD, the work is happening I am sure one day we will come to this world with a great invention in an electrical field, which may create a revolution.

Iam not from the electrical field, I have no support in the beginning, I don't have clarity about my success, I am failing again and again, I am losing my investment again and again, I am disturbed my all other works and working on this concept from last 6months, yet I can't able to see any progress. Iam failed at least 5–6 times every day. Until when I meet a professor & his Ph.D students who took serious about my concept, I don't know how important it was.

> *"Habit is a Cable; we weave a thread of it each day, and become so strong we cannot break it".*
>
> *– Horace Mann*

I not clear about my success, but Iam clear about my concept, I trusted that concept to make it happen, I am ready to fail even for next 1year or even for next 10years and more but I am not ready to quite my trails. Because failing repeatedly making me to learn something new about the mechanism.

I believed, failing is a part of success, as I fail more I am moving a step ahead in making my concept into reality. Iam sure Iam learned. when I fail a new trial in connecting the circuit, I learned it's not the right way to do so, then will rise with a reason why this circuit failed in the way I connected. So, I learned many ways in which the circuit doest works, so there are no options now, I will find a new way; one day it works if I will be keep trying some other way.

I understood, by seeing Successful peoples who failed many time before getting success in their life, they learned to fail; and they accepted the failure as a part of success. Here the story of ELON MUSK

I felt it is necessary to know about Elon Musk, who is the most powerful person on the earth, will change the view of the world & humanity. Iam sure he is going to impact the world with his innovative thoughts & actions, everyone has thoughts like Elon Musk, but who are ready to make them into actions? So it's necessary to know about a man who learned to fail for becoming success.

> "Success is going from failure to failure without loss of enthusiasm".
>
> – Winston Churchill

We all know Elon Musk as the brainiac, who also happens to be worth almost $12 billion. But, before being a billionaire, his only assets were his brain and *a vision to change the world and humanity. His ideas, initially termed dreams by many, have turned into realities.* He could be regarded as a serial entrepreneur, an entrepreneur who continuously comes up with new ideas and starts new businesses, instead, we have coined a new term for him: 'parallel entrepreneur'. He is someone who has implemented his ideas parallel in more than one industry. He has not just started these businesses, but revolutionized every industry he has touched:

- E-Cash (PayPal),
- Electric Cars (Tesla),
- Rocket Technology (SpaceX)
- Energy Services (SolarCity).

But before reaching on top of one of the tallest mountains, Elon Musk had to go through many lows, failures and problems. But he is on top of the mountain because he believed, Failures make a man successful, the greater failures you overcome the greater man & successful man you become.

> "If something is important enough you should try,
> Even if the probable outcome is failure".
>
> – Elon Musk

Two guys by name jack canfield & mark victor wrote a book about inspiration stories, and they approached the publisher to publish their book. They thought it would happen as they think, but the 1st publisher said No, the 2nd said No, 33nd said NO, but 34th said Yes! After failing 33 times they launched the book – it was: Chicken Soup for the soul, this series made more than 120 million copies and stood as one of the best book ever in the history. Such a great success they got after failing 33 times to publish their book. The one more trail costs 120 Million copies of success;

> *"Failure is never an end to anyone,*
> *Only the number of trails matters and the success is for sure".*
>
> *– Dr. San Bharath*

With the self discipline habit you get control regarding the works or acts you do, the self discipline habit is a ability of getting a clear task to do, what you must do and when you must do, whether you are do it for longer or you will give-up in between. When you are with clarity about a work or an acts whether you really want or not, then you can apply a never give-up habit to that.

> *Chain of habit is too light to be felt until they are*
> *Too heavy to be broken.*
>
> *– Warren Buffett*

Break Bad Habits, Build Good Habits

When you are the result of your habit, for seeking a good result, you should be nurtured with a good habit. As you change your habit, you can change your future. The result what you are now is the result of your old habits, your old thoughts and your old intentions; if you are living a satisfied life & the life which you are supposed to live, then there is no need to change your habits, thoughts & intentions let them continue and hold them for longer period, if you are not what you are & what you are not supposed to be, then cultivate a new habits, thoughts & intentions which can make you what you want & supposed to become.

> *"We first make our habits, and then our habits make us".*
>
> *– John Dryden*

The habit is an addiction of making a regular thing repeatedly without your notice, what you do regularly you will become again & again. First you will make a habit, then that habit will make you as an addiction force. The addiction is stronger force which has a power to make you daily with a good habit, and to break you daily with a bad habit.

It is good news to you, you can learn a good habit and you can unlearn a bad habit too, the unlearning of a bad habit can be done with ignoring of doing that habit daily and replacing that with a good habit which can make you progressively and help you in achieving what you want in your life. All habits can be learned & even unlearned, so there is no special rehabilitation course or a special psychological counseling is required to unlearn bad habit, its needed your time to think and understand your bad habits and replace it will good one.

> *"Healthy habits were learned in the same way, as unhealthy ones through practice"*
>
> – Wayne Dyer

The intention less habits can be unlearned easily; most of the bad habits were intention less, which was done by just for fun or for entertainment with no intention. A strong intention can make the habit strong, if the intention is logical which was formed by a reason; a reason to become successful, a reason to become millionaire for living a rich life, if you have a strong intention of becoming a successful & richer you will develop a new & good habit which is required for achieving them as a default. You just need to be cautious about what you want. If you are clear with what you want & you accept what you want honestly to yourself, which will make you to think about that; this thinking will make your habit & that habit will make you.

> *"You cannot change your future; you can change your habits. And surely your habits will change your future".*
>
> – APJ Abdul kalam

Old Habits Don't Bring New Results

It's hard to kill the old habits; old habits should be either killed or insulted with ignorance. Old habits are like un-leaving you as they make friendship with you they try to remain with you forever. It may be good or bad habit, if once it's a habit it stays longer with you unless you hold it.

This is reasoned because the habits were formed in the basal ganglia of your brain, so it remembers the nerve pathway which was fired on. Here is the place where the information and data of the habit were stored and restored. The habit remembers stronger as you do repeatedly again and again, the nerve pathway remembers the information deeper and more with more repetition.

> *"When someone puts an end to something, it doesn't mean that he gave up, it means that thing is not taking him anywhere."*
>
> *– Michael Bassey Johnson*

The unwanted, bad, ill habits can be removed from the basal ganglia by forgetting and removing completely or by insulting it, the insulting to the habit was getting control over yourself and ignoring the habit on your regular time. If you ignore that for next 3months, the habit will be fully insulted and lowers its power or impact on you.

When you are conscious about yourself, when you come to know that your habits were making you to be what you are, take control and responsibility for your life, you will notice that, changing a single habit can change your life. Moving from an old habit cannot repeat the same result, the result will changes.

Don't expect the new results and new life with your old habits. You are no more moving forward in your life with your old habits, the old habits will tie you to a certain chain lock, where you will be getting everything same every day with no progress, life becomes boredom; life loses the excitement of new and the fresh results.

> *"I had begun to feel that life was a repetition of the same thing; that there was nothing new either in me or in him; and that, on the contrary, we kept going back as it were on what was old."*
>
> *– Leo Tolstoy, Family Happiness*

Once you leave your old habits, you are supposed to get the new results and new life.

First Leave these 6 Habits from Your Life

1. Over Thinking (Creating Stress)
2. Trying To Please Everyone (Beggaring)
3. Fearing Change (Losing The New)
4. Living In Past (Killing Present)
5. Don't waste your time (Don't lose Your Life)
6. Putting Yourself Down (Self Under Estimation)

All these 6 habits are conquering your valuable life form many ways; if you ignore them they will conquer you completely, so you conquer them before they do. You have a freedom of changing the habits you want to do, you just need to take a responsibility about your habits whether they are making you better or making the worst.

Nothing can change nothing, even your result & the life. You should take responsibility about your habit and the results you get by them. Make an effort to make a better habit, which can make you better every day. Your results are by your choice of habits and you are made by the habits, so don't take too much time to the habit which is not improving you better. Be aware of your habits.

22

The Power

"Money, it turned out, was exactly like sex, you thought of nothing else if you didn't have it and thought of other things if you did".

– James Baldwin

The Power: Human gets the power from 2 ways:

1. Internal Power
2. External Power

Internal Power:

- ✓ The power from Conscious Mind
- ✓ The power form Sub Conscious Mind

The power form Conscious mind

"When a man is penalized for honesty he learns to lie."

– Criss Jami

It is in your control, it contains all of the thoughts, memories, feelings, and desires of which we are aware at any given moment. This is the aspect of our thought processing that we can think and talk about rationally (with a reason) after understanding. The conscious mind involves all of the things that you are currently aware of and thinking about. It is somewhat limited in terms of capacity. Your awareness of self and the world around you are part of your consciousness, the more you become aware about yourself and the world when you think and understand deeper.

> *"If your mind carries a heavy burden of past, you will experience more of the same. The past perpetuates itself through lack of presence. The quality of your consciousness at this moment is what shapes the future."*
>
> *– Eckhart Tolle*

So it is mainly considered about understanding, rational thinking or logical thinking.

Power of understanding

> *"Any fool can know. The point is to understand."*
>
> *– Albert Einstein*

Understanding is the Gist of concept, accepted by your conscious mind; it is a theory, concept and practical oriented.

The more you understand that much more you get aware of living in this world. There is nothing in life is to be feared or worried, it is only to be understood. As you understand more, you get conquer more control. You can get control even on judgment, those who understand no need to judge, and those who judge can never understand the concept.

You can break all the pains and struggling of your life by getting understood, as you can't break the huge wood by your hand madly, you have to understand it should be cut by the tool like an axe or a wood cutter blade.

> *"Knowing is, not understanding. There is a great difference between knowing and understanding: you can know a lot about something and not really understand it."*
>
> *– Charles Kettering*

Power of rational thinking

> *"Reasoning is hard to practice compared to the capacity of sentiments, but when practiced, it opens up new gateways of perception."*
>
> *– Abhijit Naskar*

Thinking rationally can only make you an intelligent, because it is a thought process which has to get practiced from your mindfulness. The complete mind should be involved in thinking rationally.

A rational thinking is the solution for all the challenged which you face in your life and which you are going to face in your future. A rational thinking has an ability to imagine the consequence and the reactions of your thinking; when you are capable of rationality, you will be aware of all conscious level challenges.

You are here because of your thinking; you will be there where you want to be, by your rational thinking;

> *"Intelligent men do not decide any subject until they have carefully examined both or all sides of it. Fools, cowards, and those too lazy to think, accept blindly, without examination, dogmas and doctrines imposed upon them in childhood by their parents, priests, and teachers, when their minds were immature and they could not reason."*
>
> *– James Hervey Johnson*

Power form Sub Conscious Mind

The subconscious mind is the powerful system and weapon which was given to the human race, which is a key for everything in your life. Learn how to activate and create a communication between the conscious and the subconscious minds. It is a powerful system which can bring everything you desires in your life. It will make you successful and billionaire too.

> "All of us have our own inner fears, beliefs, opinions. These inner assumptions rule and govern our lives. A suggestion has no power in and of itself. Its power arises from the fact that you accept it mentally."
>
> – Joseph Murphy

The subconscious mind considerably notes your beliefs, previous experience, memories, talent and your skills. In a research it was said, a great scientist Albert Einstein used not more than 10% of his brain in his complete life. The most part of the brain is Subconscious mind.

As an autonomic system and semi-autonomic system like respiration, the sub-conscious mind too works. The breathing is autonomic process of respiration, it will be automatic even in your sleep, it will be continuous process, it also has a semi – autonomic system that we can control the breath for a while, when fall in the water we will take control over our breath and hold for a while, while doctor checking the chest murmurs with stethoscope we take a deep and long breath. Likewise your sub-conscious mind also an autonomic, it will be continuously active ever, but when you want to give any suggestions through your conscious mind it can consider and accepts.

Sub conscious mind and 6th Sense

> "Never finish a negative statement; reverse it immediately, and wonders will happen in your life."
>
> – Joseph Murphy

Sometimes we feel something good or bad will happen this was considered by some unexpected thoughts in our minds. This is because of an indicator system. It constantly monitors the information coming from the senses for good and bad.

It would communicate *that* information to the conscious mind, in the form of a thought or a dream. The communication between your conscious and sub conscious minds were 2 ways, Can Give and Can Get.

> *"The only path by which another person can upset you is through your own thought."*
>
> *– Joseph Murphy*

Communicating to your subconscious mind

First you believe what you want clearly without any conflicts in it, and then start suggesting your subconscious mind by repeatedly telling what you want, again and again.

> *"Remember, you have the capacity to choose. Choose life! Choose love! Choose health!"*
>
> *– Joseph Murphy*

Sub conscious mind-don't know the truth

No matter what you believe, your sub conscious mind will believe your conscious mind and it will assume that as true. "If a man was worried about the money and thinking that he will get loss in his business and what to do if I get loss"? His sub-conscious mind will accept his worries as truth and it will help his in bringing his worries and loss to him in reality. If you feed negative suggestion to your SCM, your life will become like an Auto-Immune Disorder Condition. It means destructing yourself with your own weapon – SCM.

As your S.C.M doesn't differentiate the difference between the positive & negative, good or bad, rich or poor, health or disease etc., so remove all the negative, bad, poor and diseased thoughts from your conscious mind. And let your conscious mind be filled only with the beneficiary and positive thoughts what you need in your life. So the SCM can take them from you conscious mind and materialize to your real life. Conscious mind is like a raw material; keep only the positive thought in it, don't ever allow or store any negative thoughts in it.

Sub-conscious doesn't know what your conscious mind wants, it observes the conscious mind and it consider what was repeated the most in your mind as priority. If you want to get a well educated, intelligent & beautiful wife in your life, if you keep thinking this repeatedly, no matter whom you are and where you are, you will get her definitely for sure in a considering time depending upon how much deeper you are believing to get her and how many times you are feeding your Sub-conscious mind with your repetitions.

SCM Fulfills your Desire

SCM will help in materializing your thoughts which you are considered as your desires with belief. The SCM has all the powers of universe within the mind, and it will do anything in order to obtain your desire done. It would channelize all the available sources and give the information and power to the conscious mind in a way of making yourdesire get into reality. It will be always suggesting you with innumerable creative thoughts to your conscious mind in a way to bring all your desire.

Never keep any other alternatives in your mind, if you have any alternate option in your brain, better keep them on note book, not in the brain. Don't let create any conflict to your SCM. If you have 1 or 2 or 3 options for a work, it may get confuse and does nothing for you. Keep stricken to one goal and one by one goals, let the SCM be clear and do its work on one goal then suggest the next one, only after the getting the first. Feed your SCM as your goal was the neediest thing for your life and you don't have any alternatives instead of doing that. So that desire is getting done Quicker.

"You must make certain to give your subconscious only suggestions, which heal, bless, elevate, and inspire you in all your ways. Remember that your subconscious mind cannot take a joke. It takes you at your word."

– Joseph Murphy

Ask What You Want To Your Sub Conscious Mind

You become what your sub-conscious mind accepts you to become, let allow your subconscious mind to get what you want, don't be idle or ignore about your being. You will get an unexpected life if you don't expect what you want. Unexpected life is to live beyond or out of control.

You don't get what you don't ask; you will get what you ask whether intentionally or whether Un-knowingly. If you are living with a failures and spending the more time with them you will definitely become like them this is power of influence, your sub conscious mind will accepts the influence under which you are cultivated to me more.

Keep a particular goal for your life; be surrounded with all the remnants of your goals, keep thinking about your goal and related actions only, don't miss-guide your sub-conscious-mind with a confusion of thinking an unwanted and un necessary things for your life. Make yourself to be in the association of peoples like who you want to become. Don't allow any peoples or thoughts to enter into your mind who or which creates a worry to your mind. Keep your mind free from everything what & which you are not supposed to be; your conscious minds main purpose is allowing in only what you want in your life and rejecting the un-necessary.

"He awakened to the simple truth that it is never what a person says or does that affect him, it is his reaction to what is said or done that matters."

– JosephMurphy

The imagination technique will help SCM

> *"Imagination is more important than knowledge. Knowledge is limited. Imagination encircles the world."*
>
> *– Albert Einstein*

Imagine achieving your goal repeatedly. It is based on having faith in the outcome. Not hoping that the desired outcome will be true, but accepting that it is already true.

This is the most powerful techniques in your life, when your desire is already fulfilled. Set aside several minutes a day to close your eyes and imagine your life *after* you have achieved your goal. See the results after achieving through your imagination:

- ✓ How joy you are?
- ✓ How do you act?
- ✓ How are you feeling?
- ✓ What are you doing?
- ✓ What lifestyle you were living?

Imagination is like masking technique, if you imagine repeatedly and feel how you will be after achieving your certain success, your SCM will believe, getting stored that reformation as reality and it will bring that life to your reality.

> *"Imagination is the beginning of creation. You imagine what you desire, you will what you imagine, and at last, you create what you will."*
>
> *– George Bernard Shaw*

Attachment & detachment technique

Get attached to your desire, which is your want to be there & go! Detach from the reality which you are living, which is your are not suppose to be;

If you want to become a general surgeon doctor, feel that you are already became the general surgeon and get the knowledge regarding them, and prepare for the Pg entrance with the immense feeling, immense knowledge & experience which you already became a general Surgeon Doctor. Detach from your reality, as longer you think about you as just a graduate Mbbs doctor, you will be locked there, so detach from that and attach to the higher one, which you want.

The sub-conscious mind can be unexplained and magical than your imagination, you might plan your life according your desires and goals, but when you get attached with your desire you can never guess the plans and movements caused by your desire and goals being in your subconscious mind, to get fulfilled themselves. Just submitting your desire to your subconscious mind is the necessary act which you can do, after the acceptance of desire by your sub-conscious mind the desires and goals will be getting manifested towards accomplishing.

Keep faith on your SCM, it will definitely unfolds your desire and bring it in reality. When your SCM receives your desire, from that movement you can observe everything around you as new, they will be accordingly your desire; your vision and outer world both will be moving to correlate and achieve your desire. You will be getting the information from your SCM which may be plans, thought, and action everything will be keep moving you towards fulfillment of your desire.

When you feed your SCM with your desire, it gives you the solution, information and creates opportunities for fulfilling it. Have you observed this in your life, few peoples were too lucky in getting immediately what they want in their life, this is not by the luck and it is by keeping a desire in their SCM. When you really decide to do something or even to go to a movie, you will be getting the information about the movie or a friend will call to talk about the movie or something else will happen. This is because when you make a decision in your SCM, you will get receiving the ideas, information, and opportunities for achieving it.

> *"The law of the subconscious mind works for good and bad ideas alike. This law, when applied in a negative way, is the cause of failure, frustration, and unhappiness. However, when your habitual thinking is harmonious and constructive, you experience perfect health, success, and prosperity."*
>
> *—Joseph Murphy*

What you think, it happens! What you speak it happen! What you believe it happens!

Be cautious about a lie which you speak, let that lie may help you in a positive way, not to down in a destructive way.

I Lost My Girlfriend by Ignoring the Power of Sub Conscious Mind

It is the time of fear by considering all the seniors, classmates and staff of our medical college for not getting low score in the internals. My intention was up to my internal score, few of our class came to know about our story, but my girlfriend is neither bothered not worried about anything but, I am!

I explained an idea to her, "lets create a story which may confirm that we both were just friends and nothing more between us and we also create a story that you have an another boyfriend who is some X, once came as patient etc." We both started telling this story to our classmates, just after 2 weeks all started believing us, because that X came into reality as a patient in my girlfriend's life, I remained just as a friend to her.

I don't understand, how could she go leaving me, as she loved me more than her fear, even she kept a permanent tattoo on her body disrespecting the family and all. But she left me by my story, which I created and repeatedly told her to tell to all; later I understood her S.C.M has accepted this story as true & believed it. So, I remain Single.

External Power

The Power comes from Money, fame – recognition, form physical strength, status. All these power help you to live your life still more comfortable and powerfully.

Some works can be done only by power, when it is to be done only by power, so use power to work for you.

> *"The measure of a man is what he does with power."*
>
> *– Plato*

Propitious Circumstance

Propitious Circumstance

Propitious circumstance is creating a most favor atmosphere which is a source of earning; through this source you can earn millions of rupee;

By utilizing your effort and multiplying your time in sufficient way of earning more income, earning exponential income;

I swear

Many were lived and left this planet in the place where am living now,

Many will come after me to replace me

Where am here,

I stay not permanently on this planet

I stay not permanently to save all the properties and aragony with me

I stay not permanently to win the cups and medals

I stay not permanently to success and to become rich ever...

I don't harm the planet

I don't allow the property to disturb by me, ill save them for further generations

I love the peoples and be kindhearted for all who come along with me for a race to win the cups and medals

I help peoples in reaching the success andto fulfill their basic needs

I don't harm planet & I don't harm people

I came to live on this planet for few days and after my turn compelte ill leave this planet with pleasure

Untill that ill save this planet and make greatly for next turners...

I Sware ...!

– Dr. San Bharath

23

If you want to become the worst possibility you can become a millionaire with 1% of your potential

"Life is short, forgive quickly to your enemies, Kiss slowly to your love & work honestly towards your dream"

– Dr. San Bharath

Our Potential to live Great life is Inbuilt with the maximum possibility; once it was proved that, Albert Einstein an average Student with minimum knowledge has used only 2% of his intellectual potential to invent greatest intellectual achievements to this earth. Research has proven that – we, everyone have contradict our potential, we are underestimated our potential to the lowest mark and dies with that.

The Brain which you are given by the god was the most miracle thing on this world its priceless & the power which your brain holds was Infinity, your intellectuality has power to get everything you want from this universe, by holding such a great power within you, what is clinging you back to stop there itself!

The brain in your cranium has most complicated interconnections, with more than billions of nerves which are interconnected, which has potential to generate more than 60,000 thoughts in a day, out of these thoughts just one great thought can make you a multi billionaire, but the thing you need here is you have to believe In your thought & keep efforts! Don't just leave a thought just like a thought, if you keep interest you can make impossible into possible!

Do you have interest to make your thoughts into Reality with your interest & efforts! Only this can unleash your potential to infinity. You have infinity number of thought which can arise from your brain, when you move accordingly; you can realize you're potential. There is no other place or a person which can show your potential and unfolds your power; you have to make this with belief on your thoughts & your efforts to make them into reality! No other power or force is there in this universe which can obstruct your intellectual potential if you believe in your thoughts & do an effort to make your thoughts reality!

You are stronger than a lion

The human body is much flexible, which can be trained to maximum extent with no limitations. You just need a right training & repeated practice to mould your muscles & its power! Its irrespective of your height & color, you can build a great body with your self-interest & some effort to build it so!

You can make unimaginable & unbelievable stunts with your body which ever made on this earth by any human, you just need to believe yourself & perform with your best effort. Such a great body you have, why you are letting your body to entrap into lifestyle disorders.

An emergency, a disaster or unexpected accidents or incidents can release the tons of energy in you, which can ever seen by you. All the energy you hold in you can be equal to some billion dollars of atomic energy!

Your abilities are more than any living being

Coming to ability there is no comparison to yourself, the ability evolves & progress constantly with your acceptance, and that ability was unbeatable with anything. You just need to un-tap all the abilities, arts, talents which are hidden in you as inbounded gift by god; you need interest to un-tap them & need to acquire some knowledge to utilize them effectively.

Hidden Power

The subconscious Mind

The ability to conquer the whole world or the ability to create a new world is hidden in you, as subconscious mind. The work of your subconscious mind cannot be imagined, it has power to conceive all your thoughts, grow them, and make them real even without your notice.

You should utilize the power of your subconscious mind- by reporting all the needy thoughts to your subconscious mind; when your sub-conscious mind accepts your report, it conceives sooner than your expectation. The reporting to your sub-conscious mind should be carefully done, because it don't know which thought is needy to you; it accepts the most repeated thoughts in your conscious mind & make you to be like that; in fact you are here right now because of the thoughts you report to your sub-conscious mind!

If you are letting your mind to be influenced by the peoples around you, to be influenced to the financial pressure or poverty, to be influenced by the failures around you... etc., and all these degrading & destructive influencing thoughts will degrades & destroy you when they enter into your subconscious mind.

All the combination of thoughts & your past influenced thoughts on your subconscious mind are the reason & force which made you to be like- 'how you are now'! You are the result of the pressure & projection on & of your mind! So be conscious in allowing only the selective thoughts into your mind, let go all the unnecessary negativity, negative people, negative influence, unproductive thoughts, useless worries, unwanted jealousy, and pseudo fears! Be far from all these, ignore all the people who let you make down by their influence on you!

You are born with ultimate potential, you are born with unique talents & unique abilities don't waste it for or by some people who already destroyed all their wills!

"The purpose of life is not to be happy. It is to be useful, to be honorable, to be compassionate, to have it make some difference that you have lived and lived well."

– Ralph Waldo Emerson

24

Propitious Circumstance

"It is the passion that is in a Kiss which gives you sweetness; that passion in your purpose fulfillment gives you Ocean of Honesty"

– Dr. San Bharath

A seed will turn in to a plant when it enters into a favorable situation; the seed (ground nuts) remain as a seed when it was kept as unfavorable situations (in a Bag or Box) it even remains as seed for years and one it will get destroyed or spoiled by some external factors, like death of seed. The seed getting contact with water and arising a root and shoot form the seed, when it place on the soil it grows into a plant.

As seed turns in to plant in its favorable situation; an ordinary man can turn into a millionaire in his propitious circumstance. A propitious circumstance contains a platform or an organization to work, for making the money on the platform. No more time is required than 6months, to anyone to become millionaire.

"Learn to adjust yourself to the conditions you have to endure, but make a point of trying to alter or correct conditions so that they are most favorable to you".

– William Frederick

Money can be earned in only 2 ways

- Selling your time and efforts as employee
- Selling the product or service

Create a Platform

For getting an income you need a platform which becomes a source for giving you income.

After creating a platform, develop your work and service, double your service for every 2 months, so in this format you can double your service for 3times. As you can increase your service, you can increase your income, hold the old customers and add new customers for your business by doubling them with the help of employees and your customers; if you already having your own business, just plan to double your service in the coming next month, think over it and keep your plan into action.

- If you can make an income or profit of Rs. 2.0 Lakhs in the 1st 2 months
- You can make 4.0 Lakhs in the next 2 months, by doubling your service, and efforts.
- Finally on the 6th month you can get 8.0 Lakhs by doubling your service of previous month.

So the total income of possibility is of making 2+4+8 = 14 Lakhs, you can make 1 million at worst with this formula.

Selection of the platform: Any platform is good to become millionaire, but get the complete information and knowledge regarding you're the business, if you can see the possibility of earning 2 lakhs minimum in the first 2 months, then you have choose the right platform.

Joining into Organization for financial freedom

If you don't have huge investment or multiple talents for running multiply systems, if you don't want to risk the money in investment & business; you can join in organization of network marketing, where direct selling is done by everyone and the profit was distributed for everyone, on multi-peoples work.

The income you get in network marketing was not just by your time & effort, but you will get the income from multiple people's effort & time;

Suppose you joined in a organization as a agent, your work is to buy a product and use it, if you get satisfy with the product you will be promoting to 2 members; let suppose you sponsored in the Organization & promoted 2 members as your team; they too will do the same work, each promotes 2 members once in their life. This is not about joining everyone who ever they see on roads, the promoting people is very much selective, who are really interested & ready to promote 2 members then only they should be sponsored;

Each person will get sponsor as an agent, and promotes 2 members once in their life; and teach them to do same what they did, and how they promoted 2 members; the cycle repeats to levels or layers & you will be getting income for number of team members multiplied with $ income;

Then the income will be

- ✓ On level 1 – your team 2 – your income = 2x$
- ✓ On level 2 – your team 4 – your income = 4x$
- ✓ On level 10 – your team 1024 – your income = 1024x$
- ✓ On level 20 – your team 10,48,576; =10,48,576x$

Propitious Circumstance

The income will be multiplying as the increase of levels, suppose if you can sponsor in the organization & promote 2 members in 1week, can finish your level 1 on 1st week; form there onwards there is no joining or promoting work for you, your work was done, you just need to teach your 2 team members to do the same for next week; so they can promote 2 x2 = 4 members on 2nd week; if you repeat this for next 20 weeks, you will get financial freedom;

This business is not about Joining, you will chose only 2 people and sponsor them once in your life time, you will teach them to do the same. Teach your 2 (direct sponsors) + 4 (second line team) + 8 (third line team). This is 2+4+8 formula, if you communicate directly with your 3 lines the duplication happens quickly;

> "A strong, successful man is not the victim of his environment. He creates favorable conditions.
>
> – Orison Swett Marden

"On the last page of this book, there is a link and contact detail about a "Multi level network Organization" where you can earn financial freedom with by attaining 20 Layers in less than 180 days if you can!"

25

Don't stay with loss & don't stop with Richness

"In the world of sex, be someone's forehead kiss, as a leader & opportunity Provider even to an enemy"

– Dr. San Bharath

Loosing and earning are like failure & success; Failure & success are the stages of life, don't fly on happiness with success and don't dam immerse in ocean with failure.

Love the journey and find the happiness on the journey where you were moving, the journey only stays with you for a long time. The success and failure will comes for a single second and goes out from your life but the journey stays for months and years with you. Enjoy the journey which you are moving, start loving the work which you are doing in your journey and store all your memories in your journey to success and save them all with your heart and emotions. "The journey which you are doing what actually matters not the failure or Success matters".

The journey which you are doing is your life, not the end point where you get success for a while or not a failure where you get failure, the success and failures are actually indicators of your journey, if you get success it indicates you are moving exactly correct & if you get failure it indicates you have to learn something and move once again in your journey. Don't high-let the indicators, high-let the journey itself.

The life will be like a wave in the sea, it don't stops until it reaches the end; if you stop at certain success step, you need to have a new emotion and motivation to start from their and to move ahead towards your final destination, so please don't let yourself to stop at any point until you reach your final destination of your life.

"No need to celebrate in success and no need to depress in failure" celebrate the whole journey of your movement with learning new!

Don't accept anything as final until you see all the 360 doors were closed. Many will see one or two doors closed and believe it as final & commit it as end, but the problem or success are not like a line which has 2 ends but they are like a point, which can gives 360 degrees angle directions. Each degree gives a new direction, each degree rise to a new door to you. There are no such problems or success without solutions, you should find clearly in all the directions by your intelligence & with patience.

A small story

It was summer there are few cats in home, to withstand the heat from summer these cats were liked to sit in water bodies like open tubs. One day a small cat jumped into tub of hot water immediately without thinking of it jumped back outside. Here that cat unable to withstand in hot water so immediately in a few seconds it came out.

The next day the cat didn't turned near that tub, it found one big pot and jumped into that, the water was cool in that, later the fire were kept under that to boil the water for bath by owner without seeing the cat inside. After few minutes the water started getting heat cat enjoying the comfort & accommodating to heat, time passed the water got boiled but the cat didn't came out finally died in that.

Yesterday the cat jumped by seeing the heat (danger) so it jumped immediately, but today the cat tried itself to accommodate for the heat and after few minutes it became weak and unable to come out and dead. Initially when the water was getting heat, the cat has strength but it didn't came out because of its ignorance, after the water was boiled cat tried to come out but it couldn't do that because of its incompetent with weakness by loss of all its energy.

In the above condition cat was dead not because of boiled water, but because of unable to take a move when it was strong. Don't ever stop at comfort zone like a cat, it may be success or a failure. Protect yourself by making a continuous moment when you are capably strong, don't wait for longer duration until you get weak or sick. Be smart; take right move at right time.

"Don't stay with failure & don't stop with Success". You are not born to stay or stop at certain place without moment. "Staying at failure makes you Anger and you destroy; stopping at success makes you Jealous and you destroy".

Keep moves, the rotating earth, breezing wind, running water & your blood never keep staying at failure or stopping at success. If they stop… you don't be…!

"The only real mistake is the one from which we learn nothing"

– Henry Ford

Move on

"Live – not to stay at failure but to move on

Live – not to Stop at Success but to move on

Stay, not to lose; but to move on

Stop, not to earn; but to move on

Grow, not to learn but to move on

Learn, not just to acquire knowledge but to move on

Work, not to earn but to move on

Earn, not to save but to move on

Breathe Oxygen, not to stay alive but to move on

Drink water, not to live but to move on

Eat, not to get energy but to move on

Sleep, not to take rest but to move on

Read, not to enjoy but to move on

Move on, not to stop at somewhere but to move on... Move on"!

Where you stop, you end there; move on until the end, your end! Keep move on, Move on...!

26

Concept of Money

Behind your every desire, there will be a consequence, just as Sex

— Dr. San Bharath

Money is root cause for suffering?

Money is a non living element created by human, which was created as a tool of exchange in the place of barter system. Which the barter system became difficulty and injustice in exchange the products & service. Money is essential only for exchange of product or service; if the product or service is not available there is no need of money to humans.

The basic use of money to related to the product and service, the root for the product making and service proving is a human mind. So all the products and services arise from humans, and the money created from that mind.

> *"You can't work three hours a week and make $100,000. Get rich quick doesn't work. Crock pot mentality always defeats microwave mentality!"*
>
> — Dave Ramsey

Money has any differentiation?

No! The money, wealth, richness are the result of man's capability and capacity to think about money. Man is earned by the efforts applied to his capacity of thinking, the richness increases as he increases his capability to think more and more! A true man knows he gets money by his products and service available, and he cannot guess more than his supply.

"Money comes and sits back on postulate to the man who accepts the possession of his mind and his efforts of actions in earning money". Money doesn't values the value of your hard work, but it values your thinking and then on the efforts, if the money values hard work then the daily labor might be the world's richest man.

So money doesn't come easily, every man should think and keep effort for earning money; your benefit should not injure or wound others. The deal of product should be equally profitable to the both who involved in the deal, with no huge profit or huge loss. When someone makes you loss, it will become an unbearable weight for your living with that injury, if you make injuries to others for your profit; it too creates same pain & burden for them too. So don't injury humans for making more money, make a satisfied deal for both.

Money is not an evil or suffer creating element, it is a piece of paper which was powered to give everything for you, it gives all the comfort, luxury lifestyle, it fulfills your wants, desires and helps to get your dreams quicker; it gives power to mankind.

Money with fools & monkeys

Fools don't know how to use the money effectively; a fool was throwing some bags of money in to the flowing river. When he was asked why he is doing this, he said, money is not giving me happiness; I am not able to buy happiness with all my billion dollars so I throw them into water.

A Man who doesn't have clarity about what he wants in his life cannot buy or get happiness with that ever. Money will not give happiness to fools who don't know his wants; money will not provide purpose to unambitious, money will not give respect for incompetent man, money don't give power to cowards.

Money was effectively used by man, not fools and monkeys with fewer brains than human.

My uncle committed to suicide by affliction, damnation and inferno

Earning more money, should make you rich but not suicide, my uncleis earning in a wrong method through utilizing his power in making fraud activities, forcing the poor to pay bribe amount and he involved in many corruption for earning more money. He became rich but he was not happy.

Money is divinity and money is god because it is the source of survival, if the source was created by the fraud and corruption the conviction makes that man to project to affliction, damnation and inferno. When the money has power to brings the whole world onto your finger tips if you earned honestly without wounding others; the same money has power to make you project to affliction, damnation and inferno if you earn the divinity money by cheating;

My uncle bought all the materials, comforts and he fulfilled his desire by his home construction with money he earned with corruption, but he never felt praised for fulfilling his desires and he deepen in admonishment and he residue of humiliation. Money became evil to my uncle for his wickedness & let him to commit a suicide and die. "Money is bad or evil for all wicked"!

Money is good for all virtuous

Money will not come to you, if you don't want money; money will not come to you, if you ignore or hate it; money reaches who respect and loves it!

Loving money is becoming money minded is not a bad aspect, in fact it's an attracting aspect of money.

When you think repeatedly about money with a feel of love and respect on it, your subconscious starts attracting it towards you. When you don't care it, it won't care you! When you love money you working for that and you will deserve it with your work.

Money is good for all virtuous, but money is evil for the entire wicked one's. Do not allow the wicked peoples to live or walk in your life, because their sin or shadow may fall on you, which can influence their humiliation to you. "Living with wicked peoples & poor people will make your life Ugly". If you are poor, come out of it and become rich first.

27

Money is not an Evil; Lack of Money is an Evil

"Money is like Sex and Sex is like money; only too much is enough".

– John Updike

The society teaches the poor, as the money is evil & it removes the mental piece and it destroys the man! This social teachings was false, the poor remained as poor because of failing in desire to earn more money. It is purely their incapability not the concept of evil or peace. In fact every poor, wants to become rich but due to lack of the secret and guts he will be remains as poor.

Poor doesn't know that poverty as a mind disease. He don't know the medicine to treat the poverty was to replace the thoughts of mind to think about money & becoming rich.

The poverty comes from false interpretations and un-enlightenment of the human mind. He remains as poor with his ignorance and by darkening his thinking, which creates imbalanced & frustrated life.

The most disgusting thing was, I saw ever: Man cleaning the human waste by entering into the drainage system; does the man really deserve this work to clean the human waste? Does he born to do that?

The man without money can lead to clean the drainage; the same man with money can move in helipads. From the birth to death, man needs the power of money. The money power can makes week man as powerful, lack of the money can makes even a strongest man to down the earth.

In fact money is the divine power to human life, it has power to capture and conquer and make whole world as your possessions, and such a power is left only to the money. Don't trap with the misguidance and underestimate the power of money. You don't get even bread without money and you can't live a man's life only with the bread to your stomach.

Lack of Understanding & Thinking remains you as Ordinary

> *"The foundation stones for SUCCESS ARE NOT: Honesty, Character, Faith, Love, Loyalty, Hard-work and brilliance; its understanding and thinking."*
>
> – Dr. San Bharath

"Lack Of Understanding & Thinking About Yourself, About Your Present Situation, Future And Future Plans Are Making You To Remain As Ordinary".

There is no need to have a master brain to become a masterpiece or not all master brain will become a master piece, more master brains also can remain as ordinary or even poor or even as nothing. It's not about the brain you have; *it's about how you are utilizing your brain for your life.*

"One who thinks about other, will remain as poor; the one who thinks about work will remain as ordinary; the one who thinks about him, about his present, future and about ideas will definitely not remain as ordinary".

Lack of utilizing his brain for himself

The technology, entertainment, politics, daily news or chit-chats etc are occupying the space in your brain everyday; occupancy of some other unnecessary information in your brain will distract you from yourself; when you get distracted more form your brain, you will be no more to think about yourself. Don't lose your space from your brain, by allowing everything & everyone in your head.

> "Rich people have small TVs and big libraries,
> And poor people have small libraries and big TVs"
>
> – ZigZiglar

The successful person & the rich is

- Not bothered about the daily news,
- Not bothered about other's headache's,
- Not bothered about someone's judgment or impression,
- Not bothered about the politics and number of votes counts,
- Not bothered about others success or failures.
- Not bothered about the entertainment as he has more entertains more from his ideas,

The successful person & the rich will be purely thinking about his ideas, his future, his works and his progress.

"Raise Your Standards of understanding and your thought process".

– Dr. San Bharath

Lack of understanding about passive income

Man remains as ordinary by working up to his retirement. He will be saving the money for the life after the retirement. Man who doesn't understand about the magic of passive income can never get the benefit of passive income. The ordinary man didn't know or didn't create the passive income so he will be struggling in earning the money for the life time.

There is a concept of passive income where you can get the income again and again by doing the work at once; the insurance agents will be getting commission from company by introducing a customer to that company by taking some insurance, the agent will be getting the commission of some % from the customer's premium every month until his insurance ends. This agent will be making the work in his young age and getting the life time passive income. Such an agent will be getting passive income even when he is on the world trip with the family or in sleep or on the hospital bed, passive income will be coming to his account.

Lack of understanding about money making money concept

There is a concept called money making money concept, the money which an ordinary man is saving in his account or in his home will gives nothing or small rate on interest. But if the money can be invested on some trusted company shares or the resources like land, agriculture, animal husbandries, and small industries etc, it can make more profitable than keeping as savings. The money 100$ you save in your home will be as 100$ even after 20years, but if you utilize that to make money with the money you have, it can become 344.7$ within 10years, and 589.5$ in 20years. Don't lose this profit by keeping your money as it is, money has power to make money but it should be utilized in a right way to multiply itself.

Lack of understanding about Time and Money

The complicated concept was an ordinary man thinks that money grows with the time. And money grows only with the time. So, he will be prepared to work for 60–65 years of his life. But this concept was not totally right and not totally wrong.

The true concept & understanding was: the money grows with time, the EMI'S, the interest dues, the money making money will be growing according the time, but the time was not the limitation to make more money. The money can be multiplied irrespective of the time also, suppose your salary was 1000$ per month then you need 8.3 years of your work to make 1,00,000$, this is related to time thinking. But you can make same 1,00,000$ within 6 months also. You can become a multi-millionaire in 6months by creating a propitious mindset through multiplying the time & effort concept. This can me later learned in detains in the coming chapters.

"The reason for remaining as ordinary or poor was lack of thinking about their progress"; keep an idea for your life and think about to make it success for becoming rich. Keep repeated thinking about yourself, about your life. If you are not bothered about yourself in becoming rich & success then who cares you? You will remain as you are, if you don't think more about you.

Someone said, "If you have no big headache then all the small headaches of others will become needles and poking your head". So keep your big headache to think about your life, your success.

> *"Richness not only makes life comforted;*
> *It makes lack of ease & brings lot of options to live a complete life".*
>
> *– Dr. San Bharath*

You Can Duplicate, Gain Success by Others

There is no need to be a creator intentionally; the creation comes when you are in the process of some or other work as a default. When you observe the companies and the products around you, there will be many companies creating same products but with their own changes, wood land company didn't invent the shoe or footwear formula. The formula of shoe was created in 13th centuries, but the woodland company was making & selling the footwear by duplicating the footwear and adding some specifications to them. Not the lee-cooper & not the Bata companies created the formula but they were crafted the formula and became billionaires.

In the same way all the other companies, there is no unique product on the world, there will be crafted products. We have many brands of mobile, every mobile was original to their company but the mobile formula was not invented by any of these companies, they may created some new additional software and features to that, the Concept of Cellular Phone technology Began in Dec 1947 with Bell Labs internal report, in which RAE YOUNG suggested the concept of HEXAGONAL CELLULAR MOBILE TELEPHONE SYSTEM, for the first time handheld Mobile phone was demonstrated by John F. Mitchell and Martin Cooper of Motorola in 1973. In 1979 NTT (Nippon Telegraph and Telephone) launched the Cellular Network in Japan. All the mobile companies which are unique but the formula was not created by them, it was duplicated. They crafted the features intelligently and become successful.

If you can duplicate the success, you too can get success. If you can duplicate wealth earning you too can become wealthy. For becoming a doctor I read the medical books and I gained the knowledge, here I didn't created the concept of health and wellbeing but I learned from the books written some other authors and doctors. Here I duplicate the information of medical knowledge in my mind, so I became a doctor. If I duplicate the information of engineering concepts in my mind, ill became an Engineer. If I duplicate the information of topics related to Civil services I will become a Civil servant. How perfectly I can duplicate that much expert I can become in that.

The attitude, behavior & skills everything we learn by seeing or observing or inspiring by someone. This is also duplication. "We learn what we see, we do what we learned, and we get what we did".

If we can get everything by doing duplicate, why everyone can't became Like Jeff Bezos or like a warren Buffet? Because they don't reveal their secret to the world, so the rich peoples don't show their formula to others. But if you learn the formula to duplicate them, you can definitely get their position.

Concept of time v/s Money

Which do you want in your life?

1. More time
2. More money
3. **More time & more money**
4. No time & no Money

If your option is to get only time, stop the work which you are doing and leave all the technologies and move to forest. Only there you can get more time to spend with yourself.

If your option is to get only money, get into a job. The job is a *concept of time for money;* if you give your time there you will get money from that. If you become software you will be paid 500 Rs hourly, if you become an Engineer you will be paid 700 hourly, if you become a civil servant you will be paid 1200 hourly and If you become a cardiologist you will be paid 20,000 hourly. All the work you are doing is to get money, but in making money you are losing the freedom of your life. You are losing your valuable time to live in making yourself to sell your time for money.

For making more time and money, create Richness and become a billionaire. If you are a billionaire then you can get all that whatever you want in your life and also you will have freedom of your time to enjoy with what you have. If you don't want time & money, join the poverty group. There you don't get time to spend and no money to live. You will be working all the time for your survival.

If the freedom & time are so precious, why most of the peoples are selling their time for money?

We already discussed about the above concept of duplication, peoples duplicate what they learn from the society. The poor learns to survival by seeing other poor's around him; the employee learns to become an employee by seeing others around.

The most painful & great disappointment to me; if there is a choice of becoming billionaire and to live the life with freedom of time & desires, then why most remained as ordinary?

The employee believes the concept of *time for money*, the employee is the man who knows and believes that only the time for money, this belief may be due to the influence of his peer group or his circumstance he is living. Such man can't understand the concept of richness easily so he will remain as employee and he will be working until his last days for his survival. The employee doesn't have knowledge of any other alternative incomes so he remains becomes an employee.

No excuse of capability: the capability of a man comes with understanding and thinking; keep some time in developing your thinking and understanding!

28

Time Eater is Poor and Time Utilizer is Rich

"Some women's greatest achievement is sleeping with a man who is rich, famous, and/or wanted by many women, whereas some women's greatest achievement is refusing to sleep with such a man."

– Mokokoma Mokhonoana

Humans were civilized to live in the community; most of the people like to live in the groups instead of living alone. People want more to spend the time with others or with anything else (technology), instead of themselves;

The developed technology killing the life span of people who are born for some purpose on this planet! Instead of that, human made themselves as search of entertainment outside to them, with others or something else!

As everyone came on this planet on own purpose, everyone's duty to fulfill that first! The first priority of life was finding the purpose and creating a meaning to that! The entertainment was highly build within the purpose, while making the fulfillment of purpose, a vast fledge of entertainment and joy were perceive by the individual! There is no need to find and run behind the entertainments.

I have much less time to be on this planet, if I spill that time in entertainment of self, I will be the worst destroyer of my life, if I involve in entertaining useless fun to others that will be a big sin to me, spoiling anyone's time is sin!

The Relation between individuals will be in two forms

- ✓ one talker- Other listener
- ✓ one Teacher/mentor - Other Learner

If I choose first option, I'll open the gate to swap the dam failure to my life! I will get nothing, if I just talk something useless with others; the listener kills his or her time, if I speak useless dam words to them. If am listening to anyone else who is speaking useless topic to both of us; it's nothing but burning my life.

If I kill my time, for unnecessary, useless words ill don't find time to learn or listen the useful words for my life. "The word has more power, talk for your benefit & profitability, hold value to your words"

In the 2nd option

If am an either of learner or teacher, my life will move towards to get success in works or goals.

I am not saying that all school and college teachers are real teachers and all students are real learners. It everything based upon curiosity, enthusiasm &self discipline of individuality (learner or teacher). During teaching or guiding someone, my concept gets cleared to myself and the information gets stored into my permanent storage;

If am a learner to some mentor or guide, the new knowledge acquires to me and this related knowledge may help me at any other related conditions!

"Begin a day with learning new, end a day with satisfaction of doing new". If I don't enter a day with new knowledge, there is no difference in entering into the new day of my life! I have very less time to see new, to do new in a new day! Let me do this without destroying my irreversible specious time in my life!

29

Living without Money?

Life without money, is hallow and ridiculous as love without sex,

– Dr. San Bharath

"**Is money** is very importantly necessary for you"?

No need to discuss this more; without money, no human can live a human life! Don't believe the one who say money is not important, because it is false. "Money gives you more support than anything else to you". I saw person eating money & she is living to eat money in all the way; they give birth to her children's to eat money.

A philosopher says – "money creates stress to you"; but now it has been changed as "lack of money will create more stress than the money" in this society. To overcome stress in your life, Earn money!

Money gives you great strength & support in solving your tasks in a easy manner; money can comforts you the way you like to live; money will boost you to move towards the unknown way; money will come with you all the way & it supports you without saying no in all the works which were capable by that. Richness was concerned well knowingly to money! Without money you cannot be Rich in this society, money is one of the most important code present in the term RICH.

Humans may change, but the currency will never change, because it is heart less & mindless. Money can be with anyone, if they earn eligibility to get it; few people will get more money from his father & grandfathers even without eligibility, money will stay no longer with them; Some will have more money by crime, theft, or fraud works, money will move from them if they hold to fear of mistakes did; money will be more & longer with the one, who is selfish, intelligent, fearless, and smart worker.

With money you can lead a great comfortable, sophisticated, respectable, powerful life; without money have to live a suffering life, "by believing that you are living a very peaceful life without any sufferings, without any pressures & stress" it is called pseudo peace! The people who lived in such a world when the currency was not yet originated have said that peace comes when there is no sort of thinking about currency, but this is currency generation; everyone on this world lives only by using money, dies without money so you cannot expect peace without having money! Money cannot bring you peace, but it can help you in moving towards the place where you can get peace!

"Everyone's common intention was money". This is open hidden secret in this society.

Money Matters More to Man

No man is said as great successful & complete living without money. No man gets things without paying money in return. Money matters more to man; no money no complete man.

Somewhere in this book I wrote, thoughts are things; yes we get all things it should start as thought first, this thought generates the power to generate the thing, and this power is Money. The thought brings money and that money brings things. Money acts as medium like a bridge between two ends. Money itself acts as the bridge in many situations of human life; it makes any moves by acting as bridge in multi directional ways in life, so I treat this as power!

If situation sometimes runes worse and you might find no direction to overcome that situation but even in such situation money helps you to overcome it, because money has power it may not directly helps in overcoming the problems at least helps as assistive in overcoming the worse situation of problem. When you feel as discomfort situation in your life might be by any or many personal reasons and I am sure money is one of them or at least as feather of your problem. The other problems might not be in your hands to save you from suffering at least be ready of keeping the feathers ready to form as a wing in overcoming the suffering if in any case.

Having more money might not help you in being peace or happy life, but having "No Money" creates suffering. "No money" attracts problem and suffering to the one who is with "No money"! The problem might come from any unexpected way but finally leads to cause suffering more! The "More money" might be as positive power, 'It is just like you don't know the value of your own body when you are hale and healthy & you suffer more when you get injures or lost your health'. Injured body or lost health creates pain and this pain creates importance of being healthy and makes to feel regret for lost health, but such feels matters nothing in lost situation.

No Money stops your moves; More Money makes your moves to more and most!

"Thought–Money-Things: No Thought- No Money- No Things"

It is not mistake to become rich. Everyone has right and opportunity to be rich, life gives many opportunities to every human being to become rich but few become and majority remains as poor. Who realize and utilize the opportunity given by life become rich, & who don't realize and utilize the opportunity become poor.

The opportunity of becoming rich will be everywhere and to everyone but many don't see them by naked eyes and many don't believe them though they can see and many don't dare to utilize the opportunity properly and many don't withstand until the end and very few hold till the end they reach richness!

The one who don't understand the opportunity and utilize that he is said as failure in reaching the complete life, though he may be in a great professional or successful person in his field, unless he become rich he was not said as complete.

Right is equal to all in becoming rich; the one who live as poor and who die as poor will be with all his own mistakes only not on the circumstance or anything else. The excuse matters nothing for his or her poverty.

The growth was called not in earning money but in earning everything. Money takes the first place in that everything. "Becoming rich brings greatness and helping others in becoming rich along with self, brings ocean of happiness and ocean of strength"! I should help others in becoming rich so you will live a complete life.

30

It's your Right to be Rich

"Currency is Like Sex, the more you have more pleasure you get"

– Dr. San Bharath

Money is an only structuring agent on the earth which you need for your whole life; No other agent can be a structuring agent next to your basic elements for existence (Food, Shelter, and Clothing)

The failed surrounding & dead system have created a conflict concept of earning more money: "A poor lives with ethics, values, honesty, happily & peacefully. A billionaire was Rich, but money will make him to lose ethics & values, more money can creates more pressure & destroys his Happiness & rich can never be Peacefully"!

This concept made a view of money as evil agent. But in fact it was not true, this was created by the peoples who has no capability to earn money & become billionaire so such peoples prefer to choose these kind of false statements and projects such concept to the society; it spreads to every human on this earth, by one of such reason we can see 60% peoples under Below poverty Line as failures; 35% peoples are living an ordinary lifestyle; Only 3–5% peoples are living real luxurious Lifestyle.

Every man can become a billionaire & live the most modest Lifestyle on this earth with the maximum luxury & great lifestyle, such an intellectual potential is there for every individual, but why 95% peoples are not trying to become a Billionaire?

Until a man thinks rationally & becomes sensible, he will remain as a slave or servant by believing all the stupid concepts created by the fools & he lives with worst possible life on this earth!

Man found that objects that were too easy & closer were not considered as valuable and objects that were too far away from his belief of possibility to obtain were also not considered valuable. Man will find many ways to compromise & under-estimate his capabilities with many considering like values, sacrifice, trying, waiting etc., & finally dies with many chain locks!

The Quality of Life with Richness

The Quality of life different to both rich and poor, being poor is sin and remaining as poor is curse for anyone. The quality of life lacks in poor. The poor can never be peaceful, he is worried to month end bills, he is worried to health upsets in the family, he is worried to house and family maintained, he is worried to future, bothered about tomorrows every day;

But there is a false assumption and poor man is peaceful and rich is not, this is meaningless sentence created by some poor person for comforting and satisfying his failure with ego. "Rich can enjoy most peaceful life and can enjoy happiest, Quality life with all the power, comfort and luxuries in the world. It is a great praise to be Rich and its most luckiest to adopt a Rich Mindset".

Allow the Best of Yourself to Become Rich

Without Richness, you cannot see the maximum possibility of a man, you cannot rise the greatest of yourself in all the means without having huge money with you. Money cannot get the knowledge, but without money you cannot get the opportunity to buy a book too, so you need money for getting more knowledge, for developing skills and improving your talent.

Without money you are a locked possibility on this earth, you can't do anymore; money can untie your handcuffs and locked chains around you and make you move ahead to all the possible directions where you want to go.

You must have more money, to get all the things which you are required to make an experiment and to invent a new thing for this society or yourself; I need money to buy a laptop to right this book and money to publish this book, and I publish this book for making more money; without money this book might not been happen to finish, because for making this book I stopped all my works and sources of income, for a while.

The object of your life is to become an extreme possibility by your development; you can project all your extremities in all the possible ways when you have more money, because money can create all the capable ways of attaining your extremities.

A person can be on freedom, when he can have all the access of touching & utilizing all the things which may be useful for making all the possible ways attaining his extremities.

Richness will assist you in many ways to unfold you in all Physical, Mental, Social and Spiritual ways; while poorness will folds you to limitedness, poorness obstructs you in many ways to fold you in all the ways with limited food & nutrition, limited opportunities to access the excellence and limited opportunities to develop or work. Only rich can access the best and Rich can live the best & extreme life than the poor.

We all got one life and the purpose of life is to unfold it to maximum and live the life to extreme possibilities; Born as poor is just a sin, but reaming as poor is curse. Don't turn your sin as Curse; let the sin be turned as Praise with your action of becoming Rich.

Becoming Rich is not Just Having Money; you need time and freedom to utilize that money

Money is not just a necessary to life, but we made it as most essential element to live a complete life. Rich is not just having abundant money in the bank accounts; its utilizing for the life in getting all the wants for living with all the possible & capable of a rich man can live a life.

Poor cannot fulfill all his wants, but the rich can utilize his money for fulfilling all his wants and become extreme possibility that he can think of becoming. The lack of abundant money can never make a poor or an ordinary peoples to live life with completeness. All the poor and ordinary wants to become the best possibility of their capability but they remain as un-satisfied and this pushes them too far from success. A rich can become all that he want to become in this world, he can get all the things whichever they want in this world. He can get a private jet and move all over the world.

Becoming Rich is not just having abundant money in the bank accounts; its utilizing for the life in getting all the wants, getting all the works done, getting all the power & materials to work for him, and getting the best in all & abundant.

So, it is not wrong in thinking & becoming rich. Keep a wanting to become Rich and allow yourself to make all necessity works for becoming Richer as possible as quick. "Don't waste or replace or sell or sacrifice your VALUABLE TIME for making you richer, don't waste your life time for making money; for utilize the money and live a complete life with the power of money you must have more time, health & you must be Young"!

Start becoming rich in your young age, and don't waste LONGER TIME for becoming RICH; there is a possible way of multiplying your effort and time and multiplying your income quicker. Utilize all the acceptable methods and advance works which can assist you in making richer earlier.

Completeness with Richness

A Man Can Be Called As Complete Successful Only When He Has Physical, Mental, Social And Spiritual Success.

- A Physical Life Wants: Needs Satisfied
- A Mind Wants (Mental Needs): Desires Fulfilled
- A Social Life Wants: Respect & Recognition, Family And Happiness
- A Spiritual Life Wants: Lovable & Peaceful Life.

Here the Richness may not directly plays an impact of directly fulfill the wants of all Physical, mental, social & spiritual life, but Richness is the key element to make possibility of all successfully fulfilled indirectly.

Without being richer it is difficult to live completely, it's impossible! The poor will live compromised and false life, accepting himself as he is living within what he has comfortable life, but it's False. Ordinary and poor are living an incomplete, incompetence, unfulfilled, un-satisfied, Un-peaceful life!

Poor cannot fill his stomach with good nutritious food and cannot have a comfortable shelter. Poor cannot fulfill his wants and desires which make him to be happy and satisfied; poor cannot give a nurtured food to his mind. Poor cannot get respect, recognition, happiness in his circumstance, the unpaid dues, unpaid rents, unpaid interests etc., will make a poor man to kill his respect and recognition; this will collapse his Happiness.

Poor man cannot affordable the love, no women with commonsense can love a poor man who cannot fulfill her needs & desires and no women want to marry a poor with whom she will be going to suffer herself in working along with him as a slave; the poor marries poor because of the social impact or family status, but the love can't live for longer days with hunger in poor hut. For love the highest importance you will become if you are rich & the non- important you will become if you remain poor and live as poor.

So don't be poor ever, desire to become rich; make a possible strive to change your thoughts and change your actions and make yourself as Rich, enjoy the real & complete life with Richness.

No more great opportunity and no better time you can fine in desiring and deciding to become Rich than now. Do work which makes you millionaire first, don't ignore the fact - Man's importance is based on his financial Status in the society.

Rich thoughts

A rich thought can help you in becoming rich; thought is such a powerful element which can make you what you want to be, even rich. The richness will begin in your thoughts.

A thought is like a seed, it may not show you an intense and immediate result of becoming a tree, it needs the time to germinate and progress to become materialized. Your thought will shape you and your financial status; so keep thinking about richness & hold them in your mind until it get materialize and comes to you!

31

You Can't Get a Successful Life Unless You Are Rich

"Understanding seals your conscious mind with Sub Conscious mind as kiss seals 2 souls"

– Dr. San Bharath

You cannot rise the best possible lifestyle, comfort, and self development without having more money with you; if you have a thought to invent something (at least a small thing) which you want to evolve to this world you need money to make such research;

Unless you have more money you not even try to make your trials in bring your thoughts, out into reality from your mind, because of lack of money and fear of poverty; if you have more money you can make more projects and see more possibilities to yourself, it makes you more & greater from the depth and inward In all the means;

"Money Assists the Talent & Skills, While Poverty Suppress Them";

– Dr. San Bharath

I am unfold as Doctor, Author, inventor, industrialist etc. for everything talent & skills matter, but I believe the talent & skills too need some money to unhide them, to show in practical; the more money I spend to buy many books, some knowledge acquiring things, more practical researchers, and I developed more skills because of spending more money on my personal unfolding; "MONEY ASSISTS THE TALENT & SKILLS, WHILE POVERTY SUPPRESS THEM"; Some rare things might happen, but it's not ordinary its really rare!

Every mind can creates daily 60,000 new thoughts on an average in everyone's mind, out of them if we can take 0.01% thought might be good, innovative, helpful to world, great thought etc., what can we do with having 6 great thoughts today which might be changing your life & impacting the world too, what can you do without having huge money with you? Can you try to make risk with getting loan or borrowing the money from interest? No, it's just not possible to make so! Or can you try these all thoughts after getting huge money after 10–20 years of your life time when you become old & help less? No, it's too not possible to make so!

This is the reason we are here! Every human has a talent; every human has at least 6 great thoughts per day, if every human on the world can make try to bring their one day's thoughts into reality, the result will be: infinity great ideas!

Your 1 year x 6 great ideas of a day= 2190 great thoughts

Out of this 2190, just 1 idea of your can change the World into unimaginable creature; there is no need to be wondered even if a man can create another earth with thoughts! Such a great things we have in us, in our mind; what we need is the money to try and make them possible with our interest!

Everyone wants to develop their life to great, but the most important thing was the money is necessary along with the wants, because the money can make support to make your wants into reality!

By all the means, money is more & most important to live a complete human life, without more money you can't live a complete human life, life will be in-complete with poverty & with middleclass income; the complete life can be see through becoming rich!

> *"You Are Correct If You Want To Become Rich; You Are Wrong If You Are Compromised To Live In Poverty"!*
>
> *– Dr. San Bharath*

It is 100% true, if you don't become Rich, you will miss to live the complete life; the joy, the happiness, the possibility, the edge, the limitlessness, the comfort, the courage etc. I am sure, at some key moments in every humans life nothing can gives such a courage & support than the money can do! Every human have might understood the courage & support which only the money can give at certain key moments in everyone's life, where nothing can works; but even knowing all the power that money can make you, develop you, support you, but yet you don't try to become Rich; Seriously! Why?

Man, who never thinks to become rich, is the man who ever killed his capabilities & possibilities of his WILL & Living the compromised lifestyle with the wage or within the calculated salary, living incomplete human life!

"Man, Who Can Get All His Wants & Makes Himself Unfold To Utmost On This Earth For His Living Of All The Life He Is Capable & Making Possible Of Living To Extreme Is Called As Rich! Becoming Rich Is Not Just the Money; it's The Most of You Becoming Unfolding to Extreme and getting the real Freedom"!

32

Becoming a Millionaire

"Everything in this world is about sex, except sex, Sex is power"

– Oscar wilde

Most people on the earth where not successfully became a millionaire, because they never thought of becoming a millionaire; if you don't think of becoming a millionaire, you can never see yourself as a millionaire in your life; most people's don't think to see themselves like a millionaire because of a wrong belief and this wrong belief can stop them in achieving a millionaire Lifestyle.

One Wrong Belief can stop your Success

Believing that success is limited for few peoples who have more talent, who can cheat smartly, who does hard worker, who are intelligent & got more PhD degrees etc., this is not true. If you believe like this you too can never become a millionaire, because this is truly a false perception most of the people accepted on this earth;

"Ordinary people limit themselves by thinking that millionaires are great peoples and they are well supported with all the extreme skills and super brains etc". No, this is not true! Wrong belief was created by:

1. False Perception

2. Misconceptions

False Perception

The wrong belief was originated from the false perception which was created by your circumstance & the people with wrong information. Millionaire is too far to an ordinary man like a far Mountain, we can't see the clear picture of far mountain, so we create our own picture which might be False. Such false perceptions will create wrong or false belief.

When I am in my schooling, I use to salute and respect all the official peoples who were going in uniforms, I believed that everyone should respect them whenever we see, like a student wish to a teacher in school. So my perception is, it's too high and tough of becoming a doctor, but when my sister got an entry into medical college for becoming a doctor I felt it was somewhat easy to become a doctor, my perception changed when I saw my sister becoming a doctor from nearer, in the next year I got entry in to medical course, my perception yet changes to smaller. After 5years I came out with a doctor certificate, I became a Doctor; but in the course of becoming a doctor I never felt any tough or hard, more over I felt too easy in becoming a doctor. Now my perception was, if I didn't choose to become a doctor I might not be passed in any other degrees because I see all other degrees as Hard & tough than becoming a Doctor.

Because this is a kind of perception arises in every man's mind, don't let stop yourself with the false perceptions and don't let yourself to live an Ordinary or failure lifestyle. If you keep a thought and step moving towards becoming a millionaire you feel no harder and no tough because it's not hard anymore than what you do daily in your life.

Misconceptions

False perception, it was formed by the observing & understanding & accepting the false information as correct from the circumstance. Misconceptions were the roots of false perceptions and Wrong beliefs; it can be considered as misunderstanding or wrong understanding-

Misconception about money

Most of the peoples who are poor they are hard workers, and they were doing all the hardness that a man can does! Most of the poor people's understand that, they are getting some wage or small income which is based only on their hard work. So, they believe that, to get more money they need to do more hard work, which makes them to be limited to this false belief; and they think its unable and impossible to them, to become a millionaire in their life; so they stop moving ahead and keep remaining there itself for ever;

The Actual Fact was

- ✓ The lowest income earner was the hardest worker and he is poor,
- ✓ The medium income earner was also a hard worker but less than him and he is ordinary man,
- ✓ The highest income earner was not a hard-worker, he is smart worker and he is millionaire;
- ✓ A smart worker is the one who hire hard workers to work for him and he is a billionaire; a billionaire does no hard work.

"So it's easy to become a highest earner, than becoming a lowest earner; it's easy to live as a millionaire than to live as a poor man"! But the misconception about money made peoples to remain same.

Formula for Becoming a Millionaire

You can become a millionaire by doing work in a particular way, where the formula gets satisfied. This particular way is exact like a calculation of 2+2=4. Whoever on the earth can gets the same result of 4; when you were asked by 2+2=? The result of this is 4 for you; the result was 4 even for me too! In the same way whoever try this formula in particular way, they will become millionaire.

Money comes with doing something by involving in a pathway, let suppose money flows like a river, whoever come and immerse in the pathway they can enjoy the water, in the same way the flow of money is like a River, you should be in between the network of passage for getting immersed by money.

When the product was manufactured at industry, the product was distributed to the dealers, distributers, to wholesaler and retailing agents and finally to the customers. The manufacturing of any product will be 30–35% price at industry level, when it comes to customer it turns as 100% MRP. So in between 65–70% of the money is distributed to all the peoples who involved in the pathway to reach the product from manufacturing to the customer; Add agents, models, dealers, distributers, wholesalers, transportation peoples, retailer shops etc., everyone gets money when they involve in a pathway either directly or indirectly.

> "No money can come out, without involvement in the pathway of money flow".
>
> – Dr. San Bharath

WORLD'S RICHEST JEFF BEZOS AN AMAZON FOUNDER

He involved & occupied the most of the part of money flow, so he became world's richest person by his Application & services. The amount of advertisement, retailer, transportation, dealer, and distributer can be paid to the Amazon Company for providing a platform of buying and it is providing service to all the customers on this earth. He makes approximately $2,489/sec – more than twice what the median US worker makes in a Week.

So the more service you provide, the more quickly you become a Millionaire. Spread your service to many and many all around through or on a platform. If you do not involve in any kind of platform or a pathway, no matter who you are you don't get any money.

The one, who is getting paid salary or wage, is also becoming a part of a pathway flow in his field and in his platform indirectly. The formula has power to cause the effect, if you involve in a platform and satisfy with formula in a particular way, no matter who you are & where you are, you will get the flow of money; no matter of your background and no matter of your talent, if you follow the particular way, nothing can stop you in becoming millionaire;

But I saw many doctors, PhD degree holders and brilliant knowledgeable persons with great talent in my surrounding remained as poor and leading an ordinary life – As a result of ignoring a particular formula to do in a particular way for becoming rich; not the talent and not the education and not the hard work will make you rich & millionaire; if the talent, education and Hard work only can make a man rich, medical college deans and professors with PhD's should be in top 10 world's richest persons list.

If the richness was based on talent, strength skills and degree etc: physically strong people, talented, intelligent, brilliant, smart, etc will become millionaire. But this is not happened, money doesn't makes you rich with just a talent or degrees!

The one who wants to become a millionaire and he does all the particular way of satisfying a formula of becoming a millionaire, he only will become a millionaire and not others; For becoming rich, you have to follow a formula in a particular way, no matter what you do. You have to do that, so that you can become a millionaire. You need not to a most intelligent person, you just need to have some reading knowledge, understanding ability and commonsense of a 15^{years} child.

Every step of becoming billionaire is done by dealing with peoples, the more and best way you deal with people's either with your platform or work or service or words, you get paid. If Jeff Bezos can become richest person, you too can become. If your neighbor can become millionaire you too can become; there are no other restrictions or reservations in this category. You can become a millionaire but you must think about in becoming a millionaire.

There is no particular field by which you can become millionaire, you can become millionaire in all or any fields, every platform has same potential and opportunity to make you millionaire; only the thing was you must follow the formula which was followed by all millionaires in a particular way. Others who were not followed remained as poor.

A man became multi-millionaire with a coffee shop- we everyone knows it as Coffee Day, who followed a formula in a particular way which should be done for becoming a millionaire; and we can see some 100's of coffee shop in our town they were remained as a coffee makers, because they doesn't followed the formula in a particular way.

Another person became multi-millionaire with a Pizza shop we all know this also as Dominos, again same thing repeated, he also followed a formula in a particular way which should be done for becoming a millionaire; and other pizza corners and makers remained as they are, because of not doing the things in a particular way (same way as the millionaires did).

The cause or reason or environment circumstance or the financial status (lack of capital) or your discontinued education or your religion etc., cannot stop you in becoming a millionaire and billionaire if you want to become; you just need to follow the formula in a particular way how it should be done. The formula of becoming rich is: as I said following the formula as every millionaire already did;

"Man must become able to think about becoming a millionaire"

– in his propitious stage!

The poverty or richness arise from your mind as a process or as corresponding elements in a way you think, to acquire richness you must think only about how to acquire; and you become! Don't pollute or distract your mind with any other conflicts or diversions.

33

To Sell (or) To be Sold

THE NUMBER 1 SKILL THAT A SUCCESSFUL ENTREPRENEUR SHOULD HAVE IS: TO SELL

"If you truly believe your product or service can fulfill a true need, It's you're morally obligated to sell it"

– ZigZiglar

If you don't sell something, you will be sold yourself for existing on this earth. The one who sell something will become a Rich & successful and the one who become sold (selling himself) will become nothing. A Steve job is the 1st sales person for I-phone on this earth, so he became billionaire; Elon musk is the 1st sales person for Tesla cars, so he became a billionaire;

Selling or being sold: Being a medical family I see most of the peoples around me are doctors, so let me tell an example of what I understood about my this; let us talk about 3 peoples Dr. Alekhya, Dr. Balu & Dr. Charan are 3 cousin of mine.

Dr. Alekhya, who did her medicine without any specialization course after MBBS, she got no opportunity in any government job or in private too in her local town, so she want to start her practice in her town with a small clinic, but in the initial level she have no financial support too and banks too not supportive, so she joined in a medical shop and practiced in a single room clinic on O.P base. She earned some amount and in 6months she started her own clinic, she engaged 2 specialized doctors by paying them and she started selling their service directly to the peoples. The clinic extended to a super-specialty hospital with 12 specialization doctors and 4 MBBS doctors working under her; all these happened in 4years, now her income is 20times more than a PG specialized doctors who are working under her.

Dr. Balu, an MS Orthopedic surgeon doctor working in his own clinic, with income/savings of approximate 80% income paid by the Alekhya to specialized doctors in her Hospital.

Dr. Charan, a specialized physical therapist, got job in the government who is getting salary which is approximately 40% paid by the Alekhya to specialized doctors in her Hospital.

Here in the above example, Alekhya is selling the service of many doctors, she is selling someone's service, irrespective of her graduation or studies; she is selling the service greater than her qualification, so she is earning more than she deserve.

Dr. Balu started selling his own service, so selling self service is limited, so he is getting 80% income paid by the Alekhya to specialized doctors in her Hospital.

Dr. Charan, became an employee working for a fixed salary, he sold himself to the job which he is doing; when you sell yourself to any organization or a company your income reduce to the lowest.

> "If you truly believe your product or service can fulfill a true need,
> It's you're morally obligated to sell it"
>
> – ZigZiglar

A sales person without vision will remain as sales person; this is the knowledge every individual have and this is poking everyone to hear that word of sales person as low and there is a hierarchy to think very much low about a sale or to sell. But the fact about selling was:

The world is about swap, it's a deal of selling & buying. Nothing is more than a swap on this world. The only source on the earth to earn money for your survival is to sale your time or to sale something; Nothing comes with nothing.

Suppose you may think that, you are not selling & you are doing a job in Software Company and you are getting every month salary- if you are not selling a product or service, it means you are selling something for money, but it means you are selling your engineer knowledge, you are selling your precious time & efforts and becoming a part of selling, your company deals with some customers, for making the project your company is utilizing you by paying some wage. The project or work did by you & other employees will be sold by the company to the customers and get profited more & it will pay some wage to you & other employees, if you are not selling something, you will become servant for company!

> *"If you don't sell some service or some product to make profit for yourself, someone will utilize you and makes profit for themselves".*
>
> *– Dr. San Bharath*

If you are just getting a wage & not getting a profit for what you do, someone will be getting profit on you and they will be becoming a millionaire &multi millionaire because of you. And not you! If you don't utilize you in a right way, you will be utilized by someone and you will be money making machine for them, but you remain as ordinary employee.

Last year, in summer vacation I went to my uncles home, one day when I went to his office I saw an employee in my uncles office wondering and surprised with emotion by seeing his double bonus cheque as a reward; he just started crying after seeing that cheque with double bonus & felt on my uncles feet with lot of gratitude for double bonus reward. Later I asked my uncle, why your company gave that cheque to that employee. He said, "he made 20millions turnover to our company with his sales in last year and our company is paid just 1.2% of his work as his salary for last year, so our chairmen thought he might leave our company and may go to other company if he gets more payment, so instead of losing him to lock him with emotional chain our company pays some amount as reward, as bonus, as best employee award, as bravo award & year of excellence awards etc., to all working labors. So, that will give a hope to them as they may get promotion to next level at least in the coming 2–3years. This hope of movement can lock an employee to stay as employee under them ever".

34

6 Months Formula

"No woman marries for money; they are all clever enough, before marrying a millionaire, to fall in love with him first."

– Cesare Pavese

Its true becoming a millionaire is too easy with just the work you do; and that work should be done under propitious circumstance. There is no need of thinking of an innovative production, its only need to create a propitious circumstance, from where you can get the millions.

There should be a source to get anything; Do you have any source whether it's small or big no matter you can modify that. if you are getting older results, it means you are doing the older things again & again; to get the new result you have to do the new thing in your business; generally the favorable business in India were traditional business, it means buying something from a source & selling that in a local area or surrounding peoples.

Here the solution of becoming millionaire

"By doubling or multiplying your sale of product & service, through increasing your efforts by increasing more team under your company"!

It's very easy to get the un-imaginable result with applying a formula of multiplication to your business; if you can't apply multiplication formula to your business, better change the features of your business, if you can't do that too see the new business, where you can multiply your time & result.

Life is short to live, instead of living the life with happiness & joy, all are running behind interest less work to earn money;

Multiply your time + multiply your effort = Multi-Millions

There is a system & organization outside the job, where it's a big ocean than ever you have seen, its multi-Level-Network-Marketing;

By listening this term many people's may feel that yes, I know this, I know everything in this, I did this, I am this etc… but if they or you could have understand the concept clearly you & just worked for 6 months you might became one of the multi-millionaire at least in the worst case.

It's a wonderful formula ever created on this earth for multiplying the time & effort and the result (income) is equal to the total multiplied time + total multiplied effort;

Suppose you have just 24hrs time in a day, of course we everyone have the same, and you can work maximum 8 – 10hrs/day and you get the result of the work you done. But through multiplication of your time you can even get more than 100hrs/day & even 1000hrs/day; and you can get result equal to that 100hrs & 1000hrs/day.

> *"its simple arithmetic: Your income can grow only to the extent that you do."*
>
> *– T. HarvEker*

The extension of income in exponential Growth is called multiplication of income: Let's calculate a small income to see the power of exponential income-

If you get 5rupees in joining in your team, if you join 2people and teaching them to do same by joining each 2, (doubling each) what will be your total people joining under you on 45th day if the doubling continues? What will be your income on 45th day?

Total Team: _____

Total you're Income: _____

One is a Small number to do a great miracle, if you alone can join the people as a team for 45 days max you may join 90 people considering 2 each day.

But the exponential team work will reach team of _____ and the income will be _____

(*** hint double 2 digit for 45times (days), example: day 1= 2, day 2= 4, and day 3= 8 ... day 45 =...? And add them all finally you get the team, and then multiply the total team with Rs 5, you will get the income)

> "The only difference between a rich person and a poor person is how they use their time."
>
> – Robert Kiyosaki

35
Financial Freedom Has No Shortcuts It Has a Formula

"Financial freedom is available to all those who learn about it and work for it."

– Robert Kiyosaki

Some doesn't accept the becoming a millionaire in 6months, and becoming billionaire in 60months because they think it as short or wrong cuts, they believe only long time & money concepts. But becoming rich is a short period is right, life is about not just for earning & saving the money, life is to live with freedom of time & freedom of money.

If you want to live with freedom, you should come out of prison thinking. Most of the ordinary peoples were employee with the thinking of 25–30 years plan for becoming a millionaire, and making them to lockup with the job they do as a prisoner for lifetime.

The ordinary mindset will be thinking like, becoming a millionaire or a billionaire in a small period not possible and it doesn't have any shortcut for success. Yes! That true, *there are no shortcuts, but the ordinary mind doesn't know that, there is a formula or law.*

If you follow the formula in a particular way you can become rich; if you don't follow that formula no matter you are you can never become free from your prison of working.

> "Money is a guarantee that we may have what we want in the future. Though we need nothing at the moment it ensures the possibility of satisfying a new desire when it arises."
>
> – Aristotle

Concept of Financial Security

There Is No Concept Of Getting Secure From Job:

THE FACT: There is no concept of secured income and security for financial support in any job or work on this earth; But my parents, teachers & the society taught me from my childhood to get a good job it will give me financial security for the life time;

My father being a central government employee, one day he met with an accident and his left radius & ulna bone were fractured, he was given 15 days official medical leave for the treatment, but he required more than 45days for his restoration of the movements of the wrist joint so he took rest for the next month also without going to work; on the next month he was not paid with his normal salary he was just paid with minimum 30% of his normal salary; he is working form 33years in his job without any interruption ever in his past 33years service, but when unexpected (accident) thing happened to him he was not paid with secured income for just 1month, what happen if he might be in an inability to go for 6months or 10months for any un-expectancy will he get salary or income? No!

There is security for the job not for the income! In any government jobs, the job is secured but not the financial security to the employee. Never think about financial security from the jobs; Job or work are purely based on TIME FOR MONEY concept, you get paid for the time you work in the job; you don't get paid for the day when you don't go to work – so there is no security for your income from any job, you get paid for your time – if you are absent or unable work you don't get paid. This is not the financial Security!

No concept of becoming rich from the job

No Employee on this Earth Is Rich except Few CEO's Of International Companies.

THE FACT: You can either become Employee or Rich, if you want to become Rich you can't be as an employee anymore, because being an employee in a job is TIME FOR MONEY CONCEPT, You get the money for your time, not for your talent, not for your intelligence, not for your efforts or thoughts; but you don't have enough time in this life to become rich through this TIME FOR MONEY CONCEPT; the time a man has is very limited.

Don't let yourself as a prisoner for the lifetime

Get freedom. Getting freedom for your life is totally with yourself. No matter what you are doing now & no matter how longer you are a prisoner, you can also become free. You have to believe this; you have the formula for getting freedom from your working prison, from your insecurities, form your financial pressures and time selling;

There is a formula for getting the financial freedom

- ✓ This creates freedom from insecurities
- ✓ freedom from financial pressure

- ✓ Fulfills your desires and makes freedom from your wants
- ✓ Gives, freedom to spend your time and more.

THE FORMULA FOR YOUR FREEDOM

FINANCIAL FREEDOM = MULTIPLYING YOUR INCOME BY DOING MULTIPLYING YOUR EFFORTS AND TIME; WITH MINIMUM INVESTMENT ON A MULTI LEVEL PLATFORM.

Create a financial freedom

It's called true wealth, not an income; the wealth should be not interlink or limited with the time, because the time is limited for all; don't be slave for your job for getting an income, don't sell your time for money!

Multiplying your income by multiplying your business: if you are getting 1000$ from your business, double your business by giving franchise at other place, so from on next month you will be getting 2000$, next again double your franchise at other places, so from on next month you will be getting 4000$, if you can double for 10 more times, your franchises will be:

- ✓ On 1st double = 2franchises = 2000$ wealth
- ✓ On 2nd double = 4franchises = 4000$ wealth
- ✓ On 10th double =1024 franchises = 10,24,000$ wealth.

If you are working with one branch, your income will be always 1000$ per month, but with multiplication, your time & effort will be multiplying 1024times on 10th doubling, so your income raised 1024times, now this can be called as wealth.

You will be not working at every branch; franchise system will work to create wealth for you! It will multiply your time too, you will be having 24hrs per day, and you will be getting income for 8hrs working when you have 1 shop; when you started and multiplying your franchise for 10th times, your franchise will be 1024 branches, and every branch works for 8hrs per day, so you get income of 8192 hrs income per day, though you have only 24hrs per day! The time for everyone is constant but the income generating time was multiplied with multiplying the franchise for 10 times doublings!

36

Perception of Network Marketing or M.L.M

"The more you learn, the more you earn."

– Frank Clark

(Multi Level marketing or Network marketing)

Most of the people remain as unsuccessful, poor & struggling for existence, on this earth for employment, for getting good salary, for getting more income, for making more profit with their will & with their talent & hard work;

In fact, they all have a solution for these problems; we can make everyone to become a millionaire on a platform, that platform was existing from past many years, but yet still peoples are remained as poor & un-successful because of their wrong perception & un-willing;

A wrong perception in society about MLM or NM was: it's about joining peoples; the core perception of MLM was not about joining the peoples anymore; it's not a big deal of joining peoples in the network, and it's not a right way understanding the business;

"Multi Level Marketing or Network Marketing is not about joining the peoples this should be clearly understood, it's about making peoples to understand about the concept of MLM or network marketing; it's about teaching people and making them to learn about the business, adopting the required qualities and developing the skills; it's about becoming a leader & making leaders"!

The MLM business strategy, the true & fact thing was; everyone has dreams and goals in their life, the dreams of all / many / few were not yet fulfilled & they know the fact that their dreams were not going to be fulfilled even after some years of the work what they were doing in their life, so they need to do the new work in a way to achieve the new result which can afford in fulfilling their dreams & goals;

All these things are known by all / many / few it's a basic concept, to get new result we need to do something new, which can give the new result, right! But only 5% people are getting done with fulfilling their dreams! What about the remaining 95%?

There is no middle class, trying class & will be try later class people, in fulfilling their dreams in their life, the fact was "most of the people (95%) want to fulfill their dreams in their life & lead a desire free happy life; they understand, to get new result, they need to do the new work. To get the big income, they need to do the big work; it's simple! Everyone knows this and everyone have tried this too, but failed & remained in 95% categories;

The peoples who remained as poor/common man/ordinary /not successful / not rich, in their life were already compromised & defeated and accepted their failure with the life!

"Why 95% peoples remained as failure in this world, because they are surrounded by failures; it's just an imbalance or inability to overcome the influence of ordinary lifestyle force by an individual"!

In MLM or network marketing also same thing happens to you; it's not about joining the business, but it is truly understanding the facts & truth of concept; and making your team to get understand with the concept and giving all the knowledge to them about the business;

Big Wrong

We can categories people into 2 types related to MLM business;

1. Wrong Person
2. Right Person

Wrong Person

The one who has no dream, the one who is not willing to fight for his dreams, not willing to fight for living a complete life; the one who is compromised, un happy, disappointed, fake, not excited about life, remained physically living but dead mentally in the past etc.,

These peoples don't show interest in learning the new things, these people's remains as how they are, they don't have will to get a change or accept greatness in their life; they were already mentally dead peoples, don't dare to think with dead!

Never, never, never, join a wrong peoples into your business, they will just destroy your business, they can destroy your business team, your upline business, they can destroy your hope, your excitement, they can kill your dreams, they can kill your faith on business and even on yourself; you can do nothing with them because they are already dead, don't try to run for financial freedom with dead team!

They are not willing to accept success or a great change in their life, so they are not willing to learn from you or from the business, such peoples can never learn, so they can do noting being in your team; so please don't allow such peoples to be in your business, and don't allow yourself to destruction my dear friend.

"it's better to work alone & slow, instead of joining wrong peoples in your team, you cannot just loss the success, but they can destroy more in you imagine, by being as a count in your team"!

Network marketing is not just a business; it's a platform of multiplying your potential, multiplying your time, multiplying your work's result & income; so choose right peoples as your partners/ team members very carefully! It's a platform for your getting financial freedom & living a complete life!

If you are a MLM prospect, if you cannot use your company product regularly and if you cannot promote your business or product with at least 2 Right people, you too be as one among wrong people for MLM. If you cannot do this, don't do MLM.

Right Person

Who has dreams & honest to his dreams to fulfill them; who are fighting for making his dreams true!

"Man with dreams is alive, man willing to dreams is living, and man fighting to achieve them is right person". Right person is willing to learn & doing work for becoming what he wants & achieving all his dreams;

Formula One: you should remember was: don't allow wrong people in your team, see in the depth of your network also up to the maximum possibility not to allow even a single wrong person;

Formula Two: you should remember was: allow the right peoples into your business, only when they can give you commitment for fulfilling their dreams;

Your un-willing to greatness is your acceptance of being looser in life; The above considered wrong peoples are wrong just because they are un-willing to become what they want to be and stopped at what they are not supposed to be!

It's not about the capabilities, not about the talent or skills, not about the money, not about the possession, everyone can become successful the only thing was whether they are willing to become or not, can make them right or wrong peoples; "where there un-willing, there is no more existing greatness in life"!

> "I remember saying to my mentor, 'If I had more money, I would have a better plan.' He quickly responded, 'I would suggest that if you had a better plan, you would have more money.' You see, it's not the amount that counts; it's the plan that counts."
>
> – Jim Rohn

Rationality of MLM

Understanding the MLM Business in a rational way, there is a reason for everything happened or about to happen; for becoming success & earning millions dollars through MLM there is a reason should be fulfilled;

The MLM should be done in a way which should be done, this is like a formula which cannot be changed, and it should be understood how & followed as it is! Without a formula it will become tough to make million dollars!

Fact should be understood- the one who understood the concept of MLM and did the work in MLM such peoples will never leave the concept though they fail in getting success in one company, and they will keep trying to change many & many companies. And finally remains as un-successful peoples with burned hands, yet they cannot able to forget the concept, because MLM is such a very beautiful concept, it's really tough to understand clearly and impossible to forget completely.

Man who doesn't understand the core concept clearly, can never do or accept doing the work in MLM; because the reason was they are unable to understand the concept of MLM. Such peoples are un-willing to make business, because of their un-ability to understand.

> *"Before you can become a millionaire, you must learn to think like one. You must learn how to motivate yourself to counter fear with courage."*
>
> *– Thomas J. Stanley*

Reason behind Doing MLM

"One is a small number, to make or achieve something greatness in the life". You alone can make small things & achieve small achievement; for every great thing & achievement you need a work of Team.

A Film cannot be making by a Single Person, It's a work of team; in such a way, and MLM is a work of team where everyone's common intention was to earn Financial Freedom. "The team is formed by a common goal oriented individuals to move together for their Individual benefit working with the team"; Here in the MLM Team work, no man is alone working for himself, though their intention is for their self development & self – success; but there work is multiplies & shared with all his team along with himself. This concept can be called as WIN-WIN concept & LOOSE –LOOSE concept;

Win - Win Concept

If you win- your team will win, if you want to win, you have to support your team to win, if you want to win, you have to take support of your team; you should be willing to both in giving support & taking support of your team for winning together;

Lose –Lose Concept

If you lose- your team will lose, if you don't work, your team will get disturbed and they should bear the pressure of your work; if you are working and your team is not supposed to work, you will fail; you will fail, not because of your team's unwilling work, but because of selecting such un-willing corpse into your team! 95% PEOPLES FAILED HERE BY THIS, BY JOINING WRONG PEOPLE IN YOUR TEAM.

The team work is happened with only the one who is moving with common goals, for getting support to your work from many, you have to do MLM.

For Multiplying Your Time & Effort

Multiply your time + multiply your effort = Multi-Millions

It's a wonderful formula ever created on this earth for multiplying the time & effort and the result (income) is equal to the total multiplied time + total multiplied effort;

Suppose you have just 24hrs time in a day, of course we everyone have the same, and you can work maximum 8 – 10hrs/day and you get the result of the work you done. But through multiplication of your time you can even get more than 100hrs/day & even 1000hrs/day; and you can get result equal to that 100hrs & 1000hrs/day.

If suppose you get 20,000 rupees saved per month, form your income/ salary for your future and you need 2crores for your life; so according to your expectation & your work it takes 83.3years for saving or making 2crores rupees with you;

Earning money is based on your effort & Time; here the effort is your work in your job and the time is 8hrs per day (240hrs per month) so for earning 2crores you need to work for 2,40,000hrs in your life (240x12x83.3). Here iam not talking about the money, but in fact about the time & effort, you are losing the precious time (life time) and your effort for making just Money?

Un-knowingly it's a fact, you, I & we are losing our life's in making money; we are losing our time, wasting our efforts for just making money; life is not just for making money right?

So we can do support each-other together and we can create a platform of multiplying our time & efforts In a way to help everyone in the system and make everyone successful in making money and live the life as we want;

Here How The Time & Efforts Are Multiplied

The MLM platform is designed in such a way, you have to get enter into the platform by someone's reference or sponsorship; so you will become as a DOWN-LINE to your sponsor and he will be your UPLINE.

Everyone in the platform has many DOWN-LINES & many UP-LINES; the team or peoples above you are your UP-LINE & the team who are under you will be your DOWN-LINE.

The main intention & work of UP-LINE is to develop the business & support the Down-line to become Successful; no one can support in such a way to a person in his/her personal life, as an UP-Line can Support in the Business. The Up-Line is just a guide for your business, the upline can Never harm a DOWN-LINE, Upline will always Help the DOWN-LINE for his success, because he knows he will be successful only when his DOWN-LINES can become Successful.

After getting sponsored by your upline, you need to sponsor few peoples who are like minded & goal oriented peoples like you; never see trying to join all under you, the joining no matters; sponsor very less as your team member. If you have choice or chance to join 2 or 3 or 4 or 6 or 10 etc depending upon the matrix the joining will be these types;

Let suppose see a business of 2 Matrix as example

Here this business is called as Advanced Binary Matrix with 2Legs; you need to sponsor only 2 prospects.

And teach them to do the same; your teaching should be effective and practical, you make the work of bringing 2 prospects into your team for Reason: to fulfilling your goals and become a millionaire; teach the same to the 2 prospects what you did, and why? And tell them to do the same with their 2 prospects.

If you can make your work in a right way: joining 2 prospects and teaching them to do what you did, for the reason why you did! Then the system starts duplicating your time & efforts.

On the day 1, you will duplicate (join 2) with 2 prospects newly; on the next day, they will do the same, repeat this for next 20days;

As we discussed above: Earning money is based on your effort & Time; here the effort is your work in your job and the time is *8hrs per day* (240hrs per month) so for earning *2crores* you need to work for *2, 40,000 hrs* in your life (240x12x83.3).

For normal job or your self-employment work, only you will be working for making money & fulfilling your goals so you keep your time and efforts in making money for yourself, and you are losing your life in that struggle, it takes around 83.3 years of time for you to make 2crores of money, by keeping the effort of 2, 40,000 hrs from your life;

But in network it takes 18 days or 180days, to reach 18th level of above explained example you get the team of more than 2,40,000 team members, when they all keep effort of 1hr for 1 time, you get the income more than what you get in your 83.3years of life time;

"Reaching the 18th level of binary duplication, it can be possible in 18 days with the technology and this android generation we can communicate the 2 members easily and teach them to so the same in next 24hrs, and teach the same to repeated the same with the next 4 members become 8 (each x 2); again the cycle repeats".

If you decide to do slow and study in 10days for each level, you can take 18 x 10days for reaching what you want for your life time;

Here you do teaching, and making your team to teach the same; you get some information & knowledge from your upline who joined 2 prospects, and you will be one among the 2 prospects and he teaches you to do what he did, and he teaches why he did! You learn what to do, and you know why to do (for your goals). After learning what to do, you will sponsor 2 prospects and you will teach them what to do (to sponsor 2 each, same as you did) and you will teach why to do (for their goals)?

This is the work of learning practically what someone did, and what to do and teaching them practically to your team without interruption and being transparent to your team members. Working for an Intention knowing the reason WHY, when you know why you want to do, you will do anything.

So it's clearly learning and teaching work, not about just joining work

Some experience I personally faced with my team members in the initial phase - Whenever I talk my down-lines regarding the business, I will hear- "sir I am telling the plan to some x prospect, he may join us, he has huge network, he is expect in some profession, he may do this or that etc.," this is not a business; always telling plan to everyone whoever they see or meet is not a business, MLM is of choice you have to choose the best peoples who are interested to become a partner, never work with new peoples; if you have option, select

2known peoples with whom you share all your ideas or thoughts will become best partner in your business and select 2 indirectly known peoples (through some other people) and select 1 from each team. You need just 2 peoples to join & this is once in your life time!

Its matter of selecting only 2 prospects and sponsoring them based on their intention and their goals list; the goal oriented peoples are not an ordinary peoples, they know the value of time & effort in reaching the goals, so teach them about the business, help them in acquiring more information regarding the business & convey the plan & strategies transparently to your 2 members team prospects the information which you got from your UPLINE'S. Teach them to do the same, to Duplicating the same information without interruption!

Never be too busy in joining more peoples, be busy in making the turnover and be busy in learning & making your team to learn how to do more productive Turnover with their team members;

Your work is to select right 2 people and work with them; not to be joining continuously, never try to do all the work by yourself – tech your team to do their work to bring their 2 prospects for fulfilling their Goals;

Joining at once

Learning & teaching is always in MLM; how effective & transparent you understand the concept of your Business and how effectively & transparently you duplicate them with your team members, that much successfully you can make a great team!

"Understand, the core of success in MLM is based on Duplicating for the reason, multiplying the people's time & efforts for benefitting them and for benefitting yourself; LEARN FROM UPLINE'S AND DUPLICATE THEM WITH DOWNLINES".

Never do Hard work in the Business, because the hard worker remains ever worker. Use the platform; understand the concept of MLM it's about multiplying the time and effort for making yourself successful as possible as early;

I Want To Do MLM!

Never do anything forcefully under pressure, whatever you do which you don't like will become a hard work for you; hard work can never make you successful. The work what you understand & like to work that an make you to enjoy the work and make you happy in the process of work and gives the successful result which ever you want;

While understanding the concepts of making money, this MLM is the best on this earth in making me as a millionaire and in making you and all as millionaires; try to understand this concept and when you really like the concept you can enjoy the work & the success too!

When you like the concept, give a reason for a Question: why you want to do MLM?

If your reason is Stronger & Honest; nothing can stop you in becoming successful.

95% Failed by this Reason in MLM for Not Doing this:

- ✓ You sponsor only 2 prospects and tell them to do the same, to sponsor 2 each. Be with them and make sure their work is done with right people;

- ✓ Beyond 2 prospects you need not to introduce any more in your life time – don't join even one extra member in the team!

- ✓ Teaching to your 2 direct prospect of 1st line, 4 prospect of 2nd line, 8 prospects of 3rd line. So 2+4+8 = 14 people;

Be in regular communicating with the 3 lines and tell them to do same upto 3 lines to communicate; don't worry about depth, don't worry about lakhs of team. You just educate your 3 lines, they will do the same! Miracle will happen!

37

Strong Image Will Receive More Richness

*"If you make listening and observation your occupation,
You will gain much more than you can by talk."*

– Robert Baden-Powell

More image, more money. Don't destroy your image with your words. Be not too open or too close with anyone, don't revel secrets which can makes you low. All the successful models, entrepreneurs, actors, business peoples and others who are standing as icon for the public were holding a great image & respect in the society; the one who doesn't have a strong image within their industry or field and in the public will not receive success. You will not have more respect and higher image with in the family and in your close circuit; this is not because of the relation or lenience you gave to the people, but because of your openness & because of lack of secret with them.

> *"You will be perish with decay of your fame"*
>
> *– Dr. San Bharath*

If you discover any secret about life that might be the great revolutionary for the lives of human, and the value of that secret might be priceless. But, if you revel that secret with your entire circle who are very lenience or close people, your will get nothing form your discovery and your secret will become meaningless & it passes on a deadly desert way. "You get nothing & lose all the importance of your discoveries and greater abilities you have, unless you have a strong image in the society".

If some successful business man or a great author or some other great personality comes on the stage and then revel this "same secret" which you discovered about the life, then the value of that secret will be a guide and pathway formula for billions of people. It will remain forever as inspirational quote for many humans. It gets a justified payment and more than that's worth, depending on who is revealing that secret to the public. It can become a billion dollar worth with a strong imaged personality, while it loses its way and meaning with an ordinary life's man.

Speak, Less Than Necessity & Reveal Nothing

> *"Make sure that your talks should be progressive and profitability to your life and don't the degrading and destruction to your life".*
>
> *– Dr. San Bharath*

Never, reveal any of your secrets & formulas of your life to anyone at any movement of your life. Don't let people know too much about you, as they know more about you will be becoming an ordinary to everyone, and you will become and remain as an ordinary man. Speak less about yourself with others and remain as smart! The less information the people know about you, the more un-reveal, hidden power will be in you, the more you get respected and the smarter you will become.

> "Most of the successful people I've known are the ones who do more listening than talking."
>
> – Bernard Baruch

All the less talker people likes to spend some time with you, if you are a good talker, and they will be until they get interested or enjoyed with your words as time passing for them, once they see no enjoyment in your words they don't turn on your side again as normal, they avoid you because there will be nothing new with you if you revel all your secrets with your over talking;

People make you to talk, until they find something interesting or new about you but one day you remain as old to them, when you get older with no new stuff they get bore about your talking and they move away from you. It's human's basic nature of seeking new & interested to them. So the entertainment fields have such a demand in our world.

> "People may doubt what you say but
> They have to believe what you have done and showed"
>
> – Dr. San Bharath

Life teaches you one day a lesson to talk less; at that stage of your life, you will learn to talk less, but by that time you might have lost more with your talks. So be smart and reduce your un-necessary talks with anyone, if you talk something it should be more useful and important to you. Make sure that your talks should be progressive and profitability to your life and don't be degrading and destruction to your life.

> Create a reality by talking with your actions; Instead of creating a great fantasy with your words. The world will listen more to your actions not to your words.
>
> – Dr. San Bharath

Let make yourself to talk with your actions more than your words. The sounds of a missile blast will be more to here than to explain; Words can just hold and extend some time to keep faith on you, but the action will make the reality and it can make sure to believe you truly and longer. Create a reality by talking with your actions; Instead of creating a fantasy with your words. The world will listen more to your actions not to your words.

"Well done is better than well said".

– Benjamin Franklin

No Need to Be Honest At Where There Is Un-Necessary

Being honesty with self or with everyone is a pride thing, be honest but don't be honest at every un-necessary situation in your life. If there is a possible or chance you need to keep quite with your silence instead of going with honesty. The un-necessary honest can bring problems and can damage your image.

Be always honest with yourself, because you know the facts & truth what you can understand about the situation or facts happen in your life. And based on your understanding level and accepting level, you can accept yourself with the honest to yourself. Depending upon your situation, your understanding level, your thought process at some particulate incident, your grownup culture & circumstance might make you allowed to think & accept yourself even when you make's some un-expected mistake. But others don't.

Truth about honesty

"Be honest to you, and don't need to be honest with everyone. Because, it is not easy to accept others or everyone with some mistakes in their life, as you can accept yourself". Don't go with honesty in un-necessary situation. Be a human, think the consequences and move according the benefited consequences to both. Do be a fool, by being honesty at everywhere, be smart and live your life happily without guilt.

"Honesty is the most dangerous habit on the earth, than being Liar". The reality of honesty is the one who doesn't have an ability to think and handle the situation in a right way, can be just an honest dump. This is not an actual pride; it is a pride in the cultured society hierarchy. In reality with a reason, it is a meaningless of pride but it is a result of lack of ability to think & handle the situation in a right way.

"Being smart is a pride thing in reality, being smart is moving according the situation with the understanding and thinking of consequences over the life". Honesty with others is an outdated topic in reality.

There is a saying in English, "Truth is a fire, which cannot be hidden for longer period". Yes truth is a fire, but the fire remains no more, not in the air and not on the fire camp. It will burn with the time, as time passes the fire exists no more, only the remnant source of the fire remains as ash in your mind. Unless you are willing to open your mind and show that ash as true, no one will believe that as true. No one is bothered about honesty of your life. Keep the remnants of ash in your mind and be honest only to yourself.

So there is no need to be honest with other and disturbing your valuable life in creating an unnecessary miserable problem with others, who cannot understand the reality, be honest with your thoughts and with your works; that can make you success with the real possibility which you can make the best for your life. Move on without interrupting your life in un-necessary problems or disturbances by un-necessary honesty with others.

A tongue doesn't get things done, where an action can do; use your tongue very less, and only where it is necessary to be used. Un-necessary utilization of tongue can lead to bring more consequences to your life.

> "Our actions are much more meaningful than words,
> A hug can sometimes express more than our words will ever express".
>
> – Catherine Pulsifer

38

A lesson from a Death Bed

I am attacked with corona virus, being a chronic Asthma & pneumonia Patient in my past medical history; I am gone though to face the severity of the disease!

I am in home isolation, I am a Doctor, my siblings & their partners were doctors, though all being doctors around me, there is an unknown fear, by an incident which was occurred on last 2 weeks I lost my 3 best friends who were died with Corona Attack, I saw my neighbor dying, who all were strong & fit like me, & they were free of any kind of past medical histories to my best knowledge.

I am struggling with asthma, pneumonia & corona Virus attack; all these made me to project to sever fever, my body temperature was raised to extreme, which I never faced & I never experienced such a huge temperature even to any patients in my life, slightly my pulse rate & oxygen saturation rate was falling down, I can see this on pulse Oxy-meter attached to my index finger.

When I kept my hand on left side of my chest to feel the heart beat with pin drop silence room, Iam not able to feel or hear any heart sounds, I can able to here the seconds sound in the wall watch which is too far from me, but not my heart sound.

The time was Mid Night 2:00 AM, I am no more sleepy; I am unable to turn any other side because of heavy body pains & muscles were in-cooperation to move; unable to lift hand or legs because of fatigue & hypoglycemic.

By 2:10 AM my lung movements were reduced which made my saturation rate yet lower, I am unable to take the breath properly, I am under suffocation all my mind & body were blank & struggling to get sufficient oxygen. I struggled this for 30 mins approx, I am sure; I am going to leave my life tonight. Iam sure, iam no more living with you all from now onwards, yet I am trying to exist; I am fighting with myself to take a breath and to move my limbs.

By 3:00 AM seeing my suffocation, my God father Dr. Sreenivas came to me and gave some medication and required treatment and started speaking with me, but I am not in a position to listen him clearly, I am slightly out of consciousness with minimal responding to my god father. He said, "DEAR SON, YOU ARE NOT DONE WITH YOUR WORKS, YOU CANT LEAVE NOW & YOU COULDN'T LEAVE NOW, ONCE YOU DONE ALL YOUR DREAMS & WORKS WITH YOUR LIFE, I DON'T STOP YOU BUT PLEASE, PLEASE REMEMBER ALL YOUR DREAMS & DESIRES THEY WERE YET TO BE ACHIEVED ONLY BY YOU; WAKE UP DEAR, YOU ARE STRONG JUST WAKE UP DEAR".

All my wants, desires & dreams came like a flash in front of my eyes, I can see no other thing, not my family, not my friends, not my work & nothing; I am seeing only the desires which I am desired to fulfill in my life first. In that desire the first one was, this Book! And I am started writing this book now on my death bed, waking with my dad's call.

On the next day I left my home, in a way to not affect any-other else in my family & society, I went too far from the people & I reached the corner of a village near by my town, there I found a half-destroyed old building I stayed in that, alone I am suffering & struggling brutally with cold & fever; I cleared all my dues with the amount what I have saved in my account, I became zero worth full, I sold all my assets & running business properties with an unfair offers on my emergency to settle every due and loans from all banks. I lost every possession I had including my car, all my values destroyed with 3 days huger, after I get well I couldn't find any way to find my life preserving any worthy!!!

I am finding a way for making my life worthy meaningfully to what I believed more about myself; with the present what I am not with nothing just as roadside man!

I am sure, the virus effect may collapse my entire asset, it may weaken me physically, it may destroy the values, but it can't destroy my desire to live worthy! Now though I may be a roadside person without a single $, and damaged physically more & destroyed values which I learned but I know strongly I will show what I am to this earth!

"I know I am in fatigue, I know I am incompetence with pain, I am moving in the hell, I am accepting this grim circumstance of mine; I will perform to get my worthy life"!

Grim Circumstance

Grim Circumstance

It is a challenging circumstance created by self for attaining extreme success, through performing like a Masterpiece;

A masterpiece is most understanding person with rational thinking & Extreme commonsense;

Masterpiece comes from the fatigue circumstance, form the unpleasant circumstance & form an unacceptable and painful circumstance.

Earth speak's

I never creates bad "He or She" on me

i created an innocents,

My creature was not false, my atmosphere which is around him or her was utmost player in changing he or she as good or bad;

But here what my atmosphere around he/she is not mine, it was altered centuries ago by few humans, So please don't blame me!

Though I am the creature, I am the nature, humans alterd, modified, spoiled & destroyed me & my atmosphere, this atmosphere was the mean point in forming a bad he/she,

I never creates bad "He or She" on me

I created an innocents... innocents..!!!

And I ever allow every one on me as innocents.. & innocents..!!!

– Dr. San Bharath

Creating the Grim Circumstance
&
Becoming a Masterpiece with Your Performance

A Grim Circumstance Mindset Can Make You To Think Practically And Perform Like A Masterpiece In This Practical World.

The Accept the Un-Acceptance & To Believe the Un-Believable By an Ordinary People

39

Become a Masterpiece by Getting Control over Yourself

"When love is at the base of something, it is a masterpiece."

– Steve Maraboli

If you don't take control about your body & mind, desires and beliefs, power and courage, your thoughts and actions, your wisdom and money, emotion and morality then the world will act as irresistible occult on you and make's you an ordinary. If you can resist against this with all the control you can take about yourself you will become a Masterpiece.

The man will leave the utmost extremity of life when he becomes a masterpiece of his life. Becoming a master piece is having the will to be a conqueror or controller of his life completely.

Masterpiece comes from the fatigue circumstance, form the unpleasant circumstance & form an unacceptable and painful circumstance. Masterpiece will be never get satisfied unless he gets all his desires get fulfilled.

> "You are the most important project in your life. Spend time, work carefully, and act with positive intent as you work to create your best self. This life is your masterpiece. You are a masterpiece."
>
> *– Avina Celeste*

Masterpiece come from grim circumstance, the circumstance contains 8powers, where a man can get down and lowered and remains as ordinary, if he does hold all the 8powers, though you get control over 7powers, the remaining 1 is enough to make you an ordinary.

So a masterpiece is the one who can conquer all the 8powers what maximum can a man gets in his life, after getting all the power, becoming success and billionaire can take very less time, even he can achieve in less than 60 months.

1. Health – Physical & Mental
2. Fame – Recognition
3. Wisdom – The Human Power - Habit
4. Power – External & Internal
5. Morality
6. Emotion
7. Courage
8. Money

The Physical & Mental Health

> *"More enjoyable moment like a hug is, doing your Hamstrings, Quadriceps, and Gluteal stretches"*
>
> *– Dr. San Bharath*

When coming to your best friends, who can be the best friends in your life than your arms & limbs. Who can be the best guide to you than your brain? Don't ignore to what you have, the healthy body and mind. Your Physical health is most important for getting better enjoyable with all the possession you get in your life, so don't neglect your health for any cost.

> *"Never be in a hurry; do everything quietly and in a calm spirit. Do not lose your inner peace for anything whatsoever; Even if your whole world seems upset."*
>
> *– Saint Francis de Sales*

The mental health, there is no force or occult pressure in this world which can disturb your mind, except you! The mind is a closed house nothing can be allowed inside unless you allow. Keep thinking about your mind's health in your mind, let not allow the thoughts into your mind what that can disturb your mind. Never allow your conscious mind to lose control over your thoughts.

> *"Do not let the behavior of others destroy your inner peace."*
>
> *– Dalai Lama*

Nobody brings you peace to your mind and nobody takes the peace from your mind, except you. The depression you feel or the anxiety you feel or the sadness you feel or the happiness you feel are not caused by others but by your own thoughts, when you think about your past mistakes, you were depressed; when you think about future worries, you were anxiety; when you think about some incidents; you were sad; when you think about the present you will be happy & peaceful. There is nothing to do with the past or future in to think or worried, keep thinking about your present target and keep living in happiness.

Don't be a fool, to be worries or depressed for something in your mind, think with that mind to find the solution and keep that mind peacefully.

Fame & Recognition

> "One thing on the world which people can addict more than a sex is: Recognition"
>
> – Dr. San Bharath

You need a great fame and recognition for your life, to live a human life. The deepest urge of the every human mind is to get the fame & recognition better by day by day. The recognition you get will gives you more enthusiasm & energy to your life, conquer the eligibility for recognition with your action.

Why you haven't tried for any NATIONAL AWARD OR NOBLE PRIZE. It's my personal assumption and feeling from my deepest rational thinking, 'I think, getting a national award is not impossible to anyone, In fact it is somehow easier than becoming a bank clerk' I believe this strongly for 2 reasons:

- 99.8% peoples will never think about to get the national award in their life because ordinary peoples sacred of greatness.

- The competition is with, 0.2% peoples. If you can become the best than 0.2% peoples you can definitely win. If can chose the most loved filed for your work, it makes no more difficulty to get a great recognition.

The national recognition can comes to you; by the best work you can perform by being passionate about what you love, NATIONAL AWARDS come to your door steps.

> *"People work for money but go the extra mile,*
> *For recognition, praise and rewards."*
>
> *– Dale Carnegie*

You are not slave or an ordinary man to work for the money, work for your recognition. The recognition & fame can make you double enthusiastic at your work, it is right to earn the recognition and fame. If you want to select the award for you, don't compromise with the award and recognition, why don't you think about the national Award? If your goal was to get the national aware with your work in the coming years, what kind of work you choose to do from now? Do you get the noble prize for the work which you are doing now or you will change the work in which you will be awarded? If you are chosen the work, then how passionately you will dedicate yourself to your work? What kind of result you can expect from such a dedicated work? What kind of personality you can become if you mind is filled to get the national Award? Keep an extra mile of hard-work with passionate, recognition comes to your door step.

Not just the food can survive you a human life, being a human you need the love and recognition in the society; if a man doesn't thinks about the fame he will either becomes a gangster or a beggar. Every human thinks about himself, in a social aspect regarding his recognition and respect as far. The one who doesn't cares the recognition can be seen by road side with nudity or as a beggars.

> *"There is more hunger for love and appreciation in this world,*
> *Than for bread."*
>
> *– Mother Teresa*

Every human is hunger for the recognition for getting the fame in the society, but without trying an excellence. Do your best with your intelligence towards the work which you committed with passionate, recognition comes to you; you can deserve the national award even noble prize, if you are willing to provide the best of you in getting the pride and recognition for yourself!

If you haven't got the greatest recognition and pride as of now, it means you haven't performed the greatest work which you could. Without performing your best with you could, you can't expect that. *"Do Your Best With Your Passionate Love Towards Your Ideas, You Will Get The Greatest Recognition And Pride".*

"Brains, like hearts, go where they are appreciated."

– Robert McNamara

WISDOM: The Human Power

You have potential in you, by that potential you can get everything you want for your life from this world. Your potential is like an Aladdin Lamp it gives everything you wants. But for utilization of your potential you need to activate that by developing your mental strength which develops your wisdom. Mental strength and Wisdom can be developed through understanding and thinking, thinking, thinking...

This understanding and thinking can eliminate the negative thoughts and discouraging thoughts like conflict, self doubt, fear of failure, sacred, lack or courage and confidence, fear of new etc., when the negative forces removes form your mind your potential can unlock from your mind. The mental strength can unfold your potential.

First you need to develop your mental strength and wisdom through understanding and thinking, and then you can unlock potential by which you can fulfill everything in your life. The wisdom is the power is an ability to cause things to happen in reality, the mind has the power to think anything, and the wisdom has power to make the thought happen.

As you develop your mental strength, you can overcome your difficulties which you can get in your mind. With the developed mental strength, ensure the possibility was for your potential to achieve the wants.

If you want to be mentally strong & with strong wisdom you need to do some needy things and you shouldn't do some un-needy things.

Needy things should do

1. Develop a Logical thinking
2. Develop the thought process through reasoning
3. Develop understanding - learning
4. Develop consequence thinking

Un-needy things shouldn't do

1. Never stress about unwanted stuff.
2. Never think about regrets.
3. Never think about pleasing or forgiving.
4. Don't hang with past.
5. Don't think about which beyond your control.
6. Never give-up mindset

Develop a Logical thinking

> "But that's men all over... Poor dears, they can't help it. They haven't got logical minds."
>
> – Dorothy L. Sayers

Remember this throughout life time, "Nothing happens magically, even the magic is also Logic". All the things happening around will be holding some concept behind. A superstition about the small pox, in previous days the peoples who attack with small pox will be isolated and sent out of the village, by telling that they made some sin, so god given the punishment. It is not a curse or punishment of god. It's a disease you know now because you were aware of the concept of disease. If you don't know the concept of disease, you may not understand the logic behind the cause of disease.

> *"You must train harder than the enemy who is trying to kill you. You will get all the rest you need in the grave."*
>
> *– Leon Degrelle*

Unless you understand the logic, everything will be seen as magical but actually in fact there is no magical thing on the earth. So, think in a logical way. Think about the logic behind your success and your failure. Do business logically, logic is not the calculation in the air it's a mathematical formula which can show you the result practically. If you can think with commonsense, you can get the logic cracked. The more you practice logical thinking you can develop the logical wisdom.

The wisdom can overcome the locus of control, which is the degree to which people believe that they, as opposed to external forces have control over the outcome of events in their lives; the wisdom can clear the vision. A person's locus is conceptualized as internal or external;

People with a strong internal locus of control believe events in their life derive primarily from their own actions; People with a strong external locus of control tend to praise or blame external factors. But the wisdom can create the balanced understanding of the locus and get control over them.

> *"He had a better mind and a more rigorous temperament than me; He thought logically, and then acted on the conclusion of logical thought. Whereas most of us, I suspect, do the opposite: We make an instinctive decision, then build up an infrastructure of reasoning to justify it. And call the result common sense."*
>
> *– Julian Barnes*

Develop the thought process

A human thought is so powerful, that power can create, invent, discover & experience and even it can destroy everything with the thought alone. So such a powerful can by channelize with processing.

Thought encompasses an "aim-oriented flow of ideas and associations that can lead to a reality-oriented conclusion". While a single neuron fires, it is an isolated chemical blip. When many fires together, they form a thought. Unlike animals and birds, human beings have very few instinctive responses and have to constantly evolve new ways and means to deal with the environment. Human has ability to think of alternatives distinguishes man from many other animals.

Thought process is a continuous manipulation of information, as when we form concept, engage in problem solving, Reason and decision making Thought, the act of thinking which can again produces more thoughts. A thought may be an idea, an image, and a sound or even control an emotional feeling. The thought process can strengthen the wisdom of brain.

The thought process can be Strength by:

- Understanding the concept
- Engaging in problem solving
- By reasoning &
- By making decisions

> *"Expand your vision and widen your reasoning"*
>
> *– Sunday Adelaja*

Develop understanding - learning

> *"Any fool can know. The point is to understand."*
>
> *– Albert Einstein*

You can only catch a small fish at the surface. For catching big fish you must move deeper. A small piece of concept or information cannot make a complete understanding. To understand completely you need to go deeper to the concept or information.

The surface understanding: it can just you know about the concept what it is, but it cannot create stuff in your mind.

The deep understanding: it is a Qualitative concept understanding, it offers the comparison, analysis, relation, creation, criticize and interpretation. For getting the

> "Nothing in life is to be feared, it is only to be understood. Now is the time to understand more, so that we may fear less."
>
> – Marie Curie

Develop deeper understanding by

- Asking better Questioning You like: WHY & HOW
- Learn creative thinking
- Understand with Reason
- Use metaphors and analogies
- Explain or teach to other, the explanation makes you move deeper to your understanding; it enables the Quantitative Stuff to mind.

Understanding – learning

> "Everything that irritates us about others can lead us to an understanding of ourselves."
>
> – Carl Gustav Jung

Learning with understanding can be called as Conceptual learning, the concept and the content of the concept can be understood deeper, such learning can create a great knowledge to the mind.

Learn with Insight: insight is the best way to learn more about a subject. Insight in essence is both knowledge and understanding derived from an "inward sight", or more simply, looking inside your own mind and body and observing it. It can be a natural process or an intentional process. The ultimate goal is to become intimately familiar with your mind and body, how it reacts to certain things and how they inter-relate to you. The key benefit to knowing your mind so well is that you can take care at something and know finding if it's of benefit or harm you.

Learn with metaphor and analogies: Seeing a sample under a microscope is a lot more detailed and focused than just looking at the sample in the hand. Developing the mind through meditation will sharpen your focus and gives you a clearer boundary on the thing you focus on.

> *"The most beautiful people we have known are those who have known defeat, known suffering, known struggle, known loss, and have found their way out of the depths. These persons have an appreciation, sensitivity, and an understanding of life that fills them with compassion, gentleness, and a deep loving concern. Beautiful people do not just happen."*
>
> *– Elisabeth Kubler-Ross*

Develop consequence thinking

> *"There are in nature neither rewards nor punishments — There are consequences"*
>
> *– Robert G. Ingersoll*

For every thought and every action there will be a default consequence, every action creates a reaction; if you are only considered about the action you have to accept and face the reaction as consequences un-escapable. So it's better to think about the consequences first before you do any activity, so that you need not to worry about the un-expected things. Make sure to yourself to be prepared for the consequence of every action you do, if you are not ready to face the consequences, avoid doing action.

> *"If you build the guts to do something, anything,*
> *Then you better save enough to face the consequences."*
>
> *– Criss Jami, Killosophy*

Consequence result oriented work

> *"Be wise today so you don't cry tomorrow."*
>
> *– E.A. Bucchianeri*

"As a consequence the result of every action will be either positive or negative to you". If the consequence is negative, better avoid doing the action though you get temporary gain. Ex: smoking the cigarette, it may temporary gives you a relaxation as a consequence it creates cancer & many chronic lung diseases more than 70 COPD'S; the consequence of cigarette smoking is dangerous and negative better avoid it.

> *"A man who does not think and plan ahead will find*
> *trouble right at his door".*
>
> *– Confucius*

If the consequence is positive, though it gives you temporary difficulty or hardness, it's better to do that. Ex: Yoga, workout, Regular exercise all these may suffer you temporarily even you may feel difficulty about them all. But these will give you the maximum flexibility to body, mental peace &

strength and a wellbeing fitness body. Though the action is difficult, but the consequence is very positive to you so better do those.

> "Choices made, whether bad or good, follow you forever and affect everyone in their path one way or another."
>
> — J.E.B. Spredemann

Think before you act, not about how to act but what consequence you may face by your action, and think whether you are ready to face them or not. The consequence thinking will really make you smart, it makes you to thinking regarding what the result you want and it avoids you to do what results you don't want if you can think about their consequences. You may avoid the misery and unexpected and unwanted challenges in your life.

Man can do anything on this world if he is capable of handling the consequence of that action; the consequence is the only force which is obstructing a man not to face misery and problems.

Example: This example was well known for the consequence as everyone must know; people are using the condoms while doing the sex with unknown because of the consequence it creates, like STD, HIV, CHLAMYDIA, GONORRHEA & UNWANTED PREGNANCY. As every human were aware of this through health campaigns and health rally programs in the society.

> "If I tell you the truth, will you be able to face the consequences"?
>
> — S. Fern

Never stress about unwanted stuff

The stuff or information which is not required to you doesn't think too much about. Knowing too much about what you don't want can create stress, it is not what stress can kill you but it's the reaction of stress does to you. Stress you feel will divert your wisdom to deadly desert.

Be practical at what you so, don't worry about a problem which you are not eligible and supposed to be worried. A worry doesn't come from bad or big problems, but it comes from the unwanted thinking about the problem.

Any problem has 2 solutions:

1. If you can solve it – do it! Don't think any more about the problem
2. If you can't solve it – leave it! Don't think any more about the problem

> *100% of things you worry about never come in your real life, So, don't worries about them, if you can do anything just do it and get relax.*
>
> – Dr. San Bharath

Never think about regrets

> *"I don't do regrets. Regrets are pointless. It's too late for regrets. You've already done it, haven't you? You've lived your life. No point wishing you could change it."*
>
> – Lemmy Kilmister

The regret is meaningless thing which you can do; it's just being a stupid in being regret with anything. The regrets is linked with past, you can do nothing to your past. Regret doesn't benefit you; it will just make you degreed to low by losing your mental strength.

> *"To be truly positive in the eyes of some, You have to risk appearing negative in the eyes of others."*
>
> – Criss Jami

If you truly live accordingly what you wanted to live, there will be no regrets, if you make yourself to life for someone else or to impress someone, which you are not, you need get regret for becoming which you are not.

> "When you choose an action, you choose the consequences of that action.
> When you desire a consequence you had damned well better take the action that would create it."
>
> – Lois McMaster Bujold

Never think about pleasing or forgiving

No matter what, happened is happened no use of remembering the mistake and pleasing for someone to get forgive to yourself or making someone to pleasing you for forgiving them.

> "Don't go into the business of pleasing people. You can't please everybody. Simply do your best at what you do"
>
> – Bangambiki Habyarimana

No one want to help you for free, if they have relation they can do it for free even without pleasing them, if you don't know them they will do that with money, but definitely not with your pleasing. Peoples are smart, don't even through one rupee in beggar's plate without expecting the praise or good for them. So, every work can be done by the talent, by your best work, by the money; no matter of beggaring them for something.

No one does anything for anyone without expecting some profit for them, no one cares the sorry or gratitude's. They want benefits, think about their benefits and provide them, the work will be done.

Don't hang with past

> "The past is never where you think you left it."
>
> – Katherine Anne Porter

Past is dead, if you remain with it you will kill your present and collapse the future. Collect the information and experience form your past, don't get hanged to that come as quick as you can from the past, don't even waste few minutes with that. Past can be a good teacher but not a girlfriend, live in the presence with the guidance of past. Past is the gift if you learn from it, past is useless if you don't learn from it, and past is painful if you live in it. So past is nothing it is everything in you how you are seeing your past.

Past can be best utilized by someone who can use it in learning, for not to mistakes again and again and go back to same position. Mistakes are common in everyone's life, but repeated mistakes can make the life to stagnant there itself. So use the past, not to repeat mistake once done.

> "Unfortunately, the clock is ticking, the hours are going by. The past increases, the future recedes. Possibilities decreasing, regrets mounting."
>
> – Haruki Murakami

The earth never moves back, the clock and the life always moving forwards, if you struck seeing in the past you cannot move forward in your life. Life has to move on without carrying the past, whether it is happy or painful you have to leave that and move on. If you don't move form the past, you miss the present and destroy your future, present is more important than the past. Have a think on that.

> "I have learned that if you must leave a place that you have lived in and loved and where all your yesteryears are buried deep, Leave it any way except a slow way; leave it the fastest way you can. Never turn back and never believe that an hour you remember is a better hour because it is dead.
> Passed years seem safe ones, vanquished ones, while the future lives in a cloud, formidable from a distance."
>
> – Beryl Markham

Past is un-changeable, don't think about what you can't change. Change your thinking, to think about the present and enjoy the present. Don't hang to your past and die in your present.

I believe who is not living the present movement, who is not enjoying the present movement they were passing the present without living; I literally mean they were dead at present in this present movement. Everyone was limited by minimal time for this life; so, let's live in the present event.

Don't think about which you cannot control

> *"If you don't like something change it; if you can't change it change the way you think about it"*
>
> *— Mary engelbreit*

There are certain things which cannot be controlled or changeable, you cannot stop the moving time, you cannot stop the aging process and escape from the death by hiding in a tunnel, you cannot change the people; you can just give a thought to think. There are many things in your life which you cannot control on them.

Better leave them. Don't break your head in stopping the time and pause the moving rotating earth. Though if you think about this for your life time you cannot, after losing all your energy, potential, age, and efforts one day you can conclude you cannot change this, this is realization. For getting realization you will be easting your time and efforts. Instead of this, you can utilize your efforts for your progress.

If you can't control something, control your thinking about which can't be changeable, and control your thinking to accept that as it is. You may not control all, but you can definitely control your thinking.

Never give-up mindset

"No. Don't give up hope just yet. It's the last thing to go. When you have lost hope, you have lost everything. And when you think all is lost, when all is dire and bleak, there is always hope."

– Pittacus Lore

You are what you decided to become or make, once you have chosen to do something it was because of your mindset at that certain level, now the situation may change you, but never change your mindset according to your situation.

If you are decided to get or make or become something, turn them as goals and sent that to your subconscious mind it will make that to happen. Never leave your dreams or works which you have chosen with your conscious mind, because you are what you have chosen to be, not to be a failure with change of situations.

The situation and possibilities will change, don't give up. The situation may kick or knock you down to the earth and closes all the doors; it's no matter, the matter is you get up once from the ground go to get kicked and knocked again and again. One day there will be no kicking or knocking, and You can't see that day, if you give-up now. As more times the life & situation kicks you, that many times you are becoming stronger mentally and emotionally towards your never give-up attitude.

The success is a matter of time; it will definitely come to you, if you keep trying! It even come to you when you stop interruptedly, but you cannot accept that success when you give-up. Keep trying for few more days. Success is yours for sure.

"Keep Going, Your hardest times often lead to the greatest moments of your life. Keep Going. Tough situations build strong people in the end."

– Roy T. Bennett

This is the principle basic law for life

"Never stop dreaming,
never stop believing,
never give up,
never stop trying, and
never stop learning."
– Roy T. Bennett

The Power

"Everything in the world is about sex except sex. Sex is about power."

– Oscar Wilde

The Power: Human gets the power from 2 ways:

1. Internal Power
2. External Power

Internal Power

- ✓ The power from Conscious Mind
- ✓ The power form Sub Conscious Mind

External Power

- ✓ Some works can be done only by power, so use power to work for you.
- ✓ Money is the ultimate power! Earn more money & conquer more power on this earth!

Morality

> *Morality can separate the understanding between sex, rape and prostitution.*
>
> *– Dr. San Bharath*

The morality is limited to an individual not for the group, if you are moral to yourself and you might be 100% right to you and it may seem to be wrong for the others, ignore it.

If a girl come and hugs a person on the road for saving her father from an accident, the intention can be known only to you and that girl, but the society is see's the action not the intension behind. When you were correct, you are moral!

> *"How can one be well...when one suffers morally?"*
>
> *– Leo Tolstoy*

Morality is an ability to think and differentiate between the right and wrong, good and bad. There is no extreme knowledge or advocate certificate can be required to give a judgment between wrong and right. You just need to keep thinking regarding that in all the possible ways. If you feel it as right, it is right, if you feel as wrong, it is wrong. The wrong is wrong thought everyone in the society is doing that, the right is always right, though no one care's and follows it.

> *"A man does what he must, in spite of personal consequences, in spite of obstacle and danger and pressure – And that is the basis for all human morality".*
>
> *– Winston Churchill*

Be moral with your beliefs, don't consider the society or any others mention in your morality. The moral view of you may not be needed same to everyone. "Morality arises from the interpretations and from the commonsense of a man"; that what arise from within is limited to you, yourself, and it may not be same to everyone. If you can able to differentiate the good & bad, you can judge and follow your own thinking and beliefs.

Believe what you feel as right, no matter what others can think, feel about your morality. Follow, what you believed and be honest to your beliefs and never do against your morality. Morality is your personal beliefs; don't change them unless you feel you are wrong. Morality should be come from the self; there is no readymade morality list which everyone should be followed, because that list must be framed by some individual only, he frames his beliefs;

> "The greatness of a nation and its moral progress can be judged by the way its animals are treated."
>
> – Mahatma Gandhi

Understanding Morality

> "Morality was probably the invention of unattractive men. Whom else does it benefit really"
>
> – Manu Joseph

All the great personalities use the morality in an extreme way. They consider their beliefs, values, ethics, purposes and their principles under a single roof and use them in every coherent consistent which they face in their life.

> "There can be as many wrong reasons to do the right thing as there are stars in the sky. There might even be more than one legitimate right reason. But there is never a right reason to do the wrong thing. Not ever."
>
> – Donita K. Paul

Make sure, your moral beliefs should be developed from your deepest interpretation with understanding and reasoning by justifying your personal and social too.

Being a human, you have to consider the basics, you cannot do sex with whomever you see on the roads and you can't justify with your morality to an unacceptable social justice, "You believe, you are giving a pleasure satisfaction to everyone with whom you did sex with them". There is a social justification everyone have a right of freedom, you can't take someone's freedom forcefully without their interest, even though you are thinking about giving a pleasure satisfaction, that is unacceptable.

No bother, if some individual doesn't aggress with your morality, but your morality should not cross the basic democratic laws framed for the human betterment. Your moralities are limited your criteria and independence.

Morality drives you to increase your worthiness, without the deep sense of morality man cannot be as man; your morality sees you, warns you, and guides you to a right path; it helps us when we are distracting from life.

> "It seems to me that the idea of a personal God is an anthropological concept which I cannot take seriously. I also cannot imagine some will or goal outside the human sphere... Science has been charged with undermining morality, but the charge is unjust. A man's ethical behavior should be based effectually on sympathy, education, and social ties and needs; no religious basis is necessary. Man would indeed be in a poor way if he had to be restrained by fear of punishment and hope of reward after death."
>
> – Albert Einstein

Emotion

Emotions are state of mind. Your emotions are the reaction of your mind with related to thoughts, memories and the environment around you.

When the feeling can make you to create your wants and desires, the emotion will help you in fulfilling your desire; Iam not telling about relation emotions, it's an individual emotion towards feelings, passion, desire, dream & goals!

Emotional intelligence

It is an ability to understand and manage your own emotions.

People with emotional intelligence are conscious about their emotions, feelings and their affects to them & to others. Emotional intelligence can be mainly benefiting to the peoples who are seeking success in their life.

> "As more and more artificial intelligence is entering into the world, more and more emotional intelligence must enter into leadership."
>
> – Amit Ray

COURAGE

> "When I discover who I am, I'll be free."
>
> – Ralph Ellison

The strength of holding your dreams and desires stronger until it gets fulfilled makes your courage;

If you are courageous, you don't leave the unfulfilled work in the middle; all rich were courageous, all successful were courageous, all achievers were courageous!

Are you?

What achievement can make you feel courageous?

_____

How much money can make you rich, have you earned that?

_____

What accomplishment can make you feel really as Successful?

_____

Emotional intelligence was consisting of 4 key elements which can help you to know further in depth about yourself. One who knows himself can be with a balanced control with intelligence.

1. Self awareness

2. Motivation

3. Social skills

4. Empathy

> "You think your pain and your heartbreak are unprecedented in the history of the world, but then you read. It was books that taught me that the things that tormented me most were the very things that connected me with all the people who were alive, who had ever been alive."
>
> – James Baldwin

40

Grim Circumstance

"The Nobel Peace Prize has always been a joke - albeit a grim one. Alfred Bernhard Nobel famously invented dynamite and felt sorry about it".

– P. J. O'Rourke

It's not a convenient circumstance, moving from the grim circumstance, it will be like moving through the hell. You can't stay in the hell by knowing that as hell. Entering the grim circumstance is like knowing what the hell is and knowing what the heaven is; you can live in the hell, if you don't know that hell is, but when you know the heaven you want to go to the heaven, and if you stop in the middle or if you give-up before you reach the heaven, you need to live in the hell, by knowing that you are in hell & you must live in the hell only.

Grim circumstance is about knowing the worst, painful and unpleasant truth; and living in that circumstance with that hardness, pain, worries and fatigue.

Let me explain: A man is living very comfortable and luxury lifestyle which he ever seen in his life, he is thinking that he is living in a heaven, and living the utmost maximum possibility of a human can live on this earth, but the truth was: his house is a small hut, just beside a big drainage system. He is living with a closed eyes and nose, which he cannot see the dirty and smells bad.

An ordinary man also living with unfilled wants, unfilled desires, living with limited knowledge, limited power, limited money, limited health, limiting potential, limiting everything and living it with closed eyes and nose.

The grim circumstance will open and show you the reality, show you the real heaven and it gives you a thought in your mind, to move from uncomforted, unpleasant living and move to destination point (heaven). If you respond to that thought, to reach the heaven by all the hardness, painful and unacceptable works you can do, for reaching the true heaven or you can limit to the hell, by knowing that hell as hell, and living with open eyes and nose, by accepting the dirty and bad smell.

So, follow few formulas for your life to adopt grim circumstance

- ✓ *Try to create your own product & company, if you are not capable of inventing, hire someone who can do that.*
- ✓ *Discover man's potential, 97% people were not using their potential for their success & remained as ordinary and poor but they have potential in them; discover their potential & utilize them at least for your growth.*
- ✓ *Plan in all the possible ways to win the war; before the enemy or world comes to you for announcing the war, you must be a winner by that time with the victory!*
- ✓ *Use people for your success;*
- ✓ *Never try to go un-necessary honesty; be honest with yourself.*
- ✓ *Be intelligent & be smart.*
- ✓ *Never revel any secretes to anyone!*

Use all resource for your success, especially use humans

If you don't use human's for benefitting yourself, you will be get involved in benefitting someone else even without your notice; the best thing was, use human for your profit without their notice & without their knowledge. Think in such a way in creating a platform in which peoples will be working for themselves & it should be benefitting to you too! Live like a Queen in a honey comb, by making all the team to do their duties, and it also should be benefitting you ever!

"People failed in utilizing their potential; At least you use them for your success";

"If you don't have a skill of swimming to cross the river, learn how to swim; if you can't learn, at least make a boat to cross the river, if you don't have a skill to make a boat, at least hire a person who can make a boat! Use that boat and cross the river and reach your destination

Accepting the grim circumstance is like being an injured lion

No animal can be cruel than an injured lion, grim situation will show you the reality; the reality was unpleasant, and painful. It was a fatigue circumstance; you face difficult to sustain your beliefs in the fatigue and suffocated situations. It is a real circumstance & is more dangerous to exist in reality. Most people are unbearable to live in this truth, unpleasant circumstance, so they become unacceptable so they are ordinary. Accept the grim & be an injured, huger lion; No animal, no weapon & no force can stop you in becoming success;

You become an injured & hungry Lion with acceptance of grim circumstance, you will fight, and you will hunt for your dreams & accomplishments!

"Talent is talent, and everybody knows somebody who has talent or ability, but they never really converted it into a productive performance for whatever reasons".

– Nick Saban

41
World Is Made By Few Performers, Aren't You A Performer?

"There is no perfect even doing sex on the first time, the betterment you has to perform again and again, you become perfect".

– Dr. San Bharath

If you are not a performer, you can't play an impact on this world;

If you creating a painting in a laptop with unlimited graphics utilizations & unlimited ways to create the paint with no limitation at all; you can take many experts guidelines & even support to create that painting!

How you will create? Will you create a plane; dull, normal painting or you will create the ever best than other on this earth? What will you try at least?

The best, the best on this earth! You at least try to create the best by using all the powers & features you can utilize right!

Life is same, with unlimited powers, unlimited potential, unlimited energy, unlimited thoughts, unlimited creations, unlimited opportunities, unlimited pathways, unlimited directions, unlimited supports etc. all you need is just your interest to play your role in performing something where you are really mean to do!

Performance VS Working

Working is selling yourself for salary or wage or profit; performance is making yourself to make something which you believed to make with an intention & interest!

The work you provide for a salary or the work you provide for a wage as return can be called as Work; but the work which you do for beyond money, an effort, for a passion; for a cause; for a great intention behind such a work can become a performance.

There will be no good or better performance, the performance itself the best than anything else; all the performers perform for a cause, with a great intention, with a self Interest, in grim circumstance, with self confidence & own risk. All these together can be consider as performance, such a performance can never get failed; once a while it has to get the intentional result!

It's not how you are performing? It's where?

You are here to create an impact on this world with all the unlimited & ultimate powers you have to perform the best, but you should know that WHERE you are performing your best at what you do; whether it's going to impact the world or not!

If your performance was not going to change or impact the world, at least any corner don't perform the best there; try the best at other slot WHERE you can sense the impact more!

Man remains normal not by knowing HOW to perform, but of not knowing WHERE to perform.

"Man performed his best, in collecting a ticket in the railway station made him to get just a monthly wage as salary for his great performance that same man performed in the Indian cricket team as capital, but here for his performance he became M.S. DHONI.

Man performed his best, as bus conductor for his monthly wage, but he performed his best in the film, but here for his performance he became SUPER STAR RAJNI.

Man performed his best, at his school age, but he was a very poor at studies & very low at his marks, he performed his best in invention, he became EINSTEIN.

Understanding Performance

The peoples with Commonsense only can understand the concept of performance; the activity performance itself tells the meaning of the Active mind behind the man; all the performers have an Active mind, which ever been struck or dead with something, the mind is stronger which will be seeking ever for a new thought, ever flexible for every activity irrespective of the field and Situation!

The performance is such an activity happen with the self interest and with the moment of "want to do" not by the moment of "have to do"; when you so something "want to do", it explains your involvement and your interest in making something which can give a result for yourself; if you do "want to do" it means it made you to understand that you like the work, and it made you to believe that you are doing for yourself for your personal desire. When you do "have to do" act creates a condition behind your action and It makes you to be understand for something you are doing this, for getting something you are doing this now, the condition is for something, when you are conditioned with 'Have to do' – for something your mind don't accepts that activity as yours or your own, so it reduces the Quality and Quantity of effort in your activity so it turns as Hard work.

When you feel, believe and accept from your inside that you want to do for yourself; that 'want to do' will creates an impact and interest for your activity and make that activity as extreme and excellence; any extreme activity performed by a man with his interest or want is called as PERFORMANCE.

Performance which arises from your Wants! Works or hard works arises from your situations! When you are doing something necessarily for yourself, as your wants & your necessity to do, your work will convert into Performance.

42

The Cultured Education for a Billionaire

> *"If you ask society to teach about a pure love, it teaches you about how to do logic less sex"*
>
> *– Dr. San Bharath*

The society is carrying the cultured education, in which it is carrying many logic less information & rubbing them on every individual; this illogical information, knowledge, and education are creating more impact on everyone and making them to be stable and stagnate to them;

In fact the darkness comes from illogicalness, you have intelligence and you have a mind in your cranium to question yourself! The answer you can get only when it is has a logic & meaning. The information and education which you learn by the society with no logic or with no meaning can be called as false; don't trap in darkness, splendid yourself into light with your Questioning.

QUESTIONING and finding a REASON are the two logical facts which can reshape your thoughts and believes; the logical concepts which you accept can make you an Intelligent and Stronger minded person.

A Triumph over Your Hidden Destructive Force

From my childhood, my father use to tell me to do HARDWORK so that I can get good marks and pass out with a good degree and I'll get a good job; I don't understand at that time what is this hard-work. I understood doing something without my interest can makes my work as hard-work. But I don't want to do the work which I don't want; I just want to do the work which I enjoy more, I enjoy in reading something so I do that more, I enjoy in playing shuttle so I do that more, I enjoy in doing research so I do that more; all what I like to do more I became that finally; I became an author as I like reading & writing, I became a shuttle player, I became an industrialist for my research product.

I didn't able to withstand in my noble medical profession as a Doctor with graduated degree, I didn't able to withstand in my job and as Civil Servant; because of the cultural education, this education made to work on a single pathway to move on a single boat. But I don't accept this with a logic, I have many choices for my life, if not this I have one more, if not that I have many more things in life;

Life is not for certainty, it's a path of journey with all your Choices, you can have many choices you can be or act in a diversified work in the life; if you want to do 10works at a time and all the 10works are of different fields, you can do if you are willing to do all, whether you are capable of them all or Not.

But when people from society were interacting me and telling the impossibility i made and tough to handle these entire etc., at some stage I thought of – I am I did something wrong which I can't handle? I answered with No. I ignored the cultured peoples; I understood the reason behind their intension: "The peoples in the society were cultured with education which made them as a limited personality, to think about only one work at a time";

The cultured peoples were forgotten their potential of limitlessness and Excellences and were living as an ordinary life's.

If you get impacted or influenced by this cultured society it can also make to be remain as one among the 95% ordinary or unsuccessful or poor or failure personality like them; the world which you were living is more surrounded with 95% of failure peoples, which can bite you and kill your intellectuality, don't let yourself to be with them under their education anymore!

All the education, information and knowledge which you got or gained will be collectively made you as you are, but you can become what you are only when you start thinking & questioning over everything you see & here in this society! If you don't think & question yourself, you too will flow along with a tide and remain as an ordinary man with compromised life!

Become a Masterpiece

A masterpiece is a Man with basic questioning and basic Logical thinking; adopt a habit of question with WHY and HOW? These 2 questions can give meaning to everything in your life; they can create a meaning for your decision, and value for your judgments;

- ✓ WHY I should do this, why can't I try greater or higher?
- ✓ HOW can I achieve greatness?

43

Building a Master Piece Mindset

"More enjoyable moment like a hug is, doing your Hamstrings, Quadriceps, and Gluteal stretches"

– Dr. San Bharath

You need to become a performer like a master piece, so then only you can become a billionaire. Along with the master piece you need to adopt an attitude of Billionaire mindset; this mindset & the working strategy was completely different than becoming a millionaires, becoming a millionaire is very easy and it's practically proven and can be practiced in your life and become a millionaire as I explained in the previous topics.

Exampling comparison of millionaire's mindset with a Billionaires one!

Suppose, for becoming a millionaire you need share your knowledge and information from your upline to your downlines; and teach them to become successful freely.

But for becoming a billionaire you need to have a selfish mentality, same action but the intention will be strong for your personal benefit here and you do nothing for free, you must give very minimal secrets and to them for the price more than the secret. Every secret or teaching cost some rate, you must tell them for your profitability & for more profitability than the worth of secret.

Billionaire mindset is unacceptable by poor, illiterate, ordinary peoples because they see such mindset as un-ethical and they don't accept fact and reality, one of the things was their unacceptability made them to remain as they are. These are true and unacceptable rational facts and Laws which can help you in becoming a billionaire.

Masterpiece Becomes Billionaire

A Masterpiece is not needed to be with extreme and super brain for becoming a billionaire but should know how to utilize the brain, it might be his own or someone's brain.

The secret of Becoming a Masterpiece

Concentration + commonsense + consistency = 3C Masterpiece

Concentration: It comes with interest

Nothing can do without interest; you should have interest in becoming a masterpiece. For becoming a masterpiece first you should be interested in becoming, showing an interest is not such an easy task.

Law of interest: when you see a thing or material or position anything regularly or repeatedly you will get some interest over that, see a billionaire regularly in the internet and follow them closely and see all the interviews understand about their words, decisions and actions regularly. I personally interested to become a masterpiece by seeing a Rolls Royce Car, Elon Mask, and Ratan TATA. I follow them regularly.

Rolls Royce car created an interest in me to become a Billionaire, the reason behind this was, to have a Rolls Royce car I must be a billionaire, for becoming a billionaire I must become a Masterpiece. The interest comes with logic; connect to your interest logically and realistically.

There is no trigger point for my interest, I don't need to think more about to become a masterpiece because, my trigger point was Rolls Royce, I kept that Photo as my mobile wallpaper, as my desktop wallpaper, it's in my wall corner, In my dream chart list, in my car, at my reading side, in my library etc., everywhere where ever I turn my eye's vision I can able to see that always; as I see that more, the more interest created in me to get that soon; for getting that there is no option I must become a Masterpiece;

Why you want to become a masterpiece, what is the strong reason which is behind your interest, strict to your reason strongly so your Interest never loses you!

Commonsense

> *"Nowadays most people die of a sort of creeping common sense, and discover when it is too late that the only things one never regrets are one's mistakes."*
>
> *– Oscar Wilde*

Commonsense is logic, sensible reasoning or simple equations. The end result is practical wisdom & acquired Knowledge. No Man, family, business can survive without common sense as a part of their accomplished strategies. Common sense will suggest change or adjustment as you proceed.

Commonsense provides:

- ✓ Safety
- ✓ Overcome fear
- ✓ Steadiness
- ✓ Avoidance & Escape from miserable;

Commonsense enables man alert to the changes in the world and we will get prepared to adapt to change in the way we do things.

> *"Commonsense is more valuable than holding degrees, PhD's; If you can give me a team of 100 people with commonsense, I will change the fate of Nation".*
>
> – Dr. San Bharath

Consistency for Longer Duration

> *"Success isn't always about greatness. It's about consistency. Consistent hard work leads to success. Greatness will come."*
>
> – Dwayne Johnson

Holding something with never-give-up attitude for longer duration with hope, until the result comes, is called consistency; it plays a key role is showing your persistence to pain and balance your faith with it.

Success may not be immediate, but it's definite; so to take the success you should stand there with consistency;

> *"Getting an audience is hard. Sustaining an audience is hard. It demands a consistency of thought, of purpose and of action over a long period of time."*
>
> – Bruce Springsteen

Concept of Richness: only 1–2% peoples are choosing to become a masterpiece. Is it tough to get a masterpiece lifestyle?

Richness is not just becoming a billionaire; it also brings a masterpiece lifestyle. A masterpiece is the, who is living in reality, living with freedom by getting what wants for his life, the real living of a human life is living with freedom of money & time. Truly if you want to live the life with a freedom of time and money, create richness & live a masterpiece lifestyle.

Everyone has choice to become a masterpiece and get the life with freedom of money and time. Becoming a masterpiece is no tougher than living as a servant for earning money.

Tiger becoming Cat

There is a concept, a tiger was trapped forest peoples and it was sold to the circus peoples. The tiger will be trained daily to do circus like a cat, and it gets food only when it do circus. Every day the tiger was supposed to do the same thing, it has been 2 years the tiger adopted the nature of eating food by doing circus.

When the animal welfare department noticed this matter, they noticed to leave the tiger into forest for living its freedom of Life. But it was 2 months the tiger cannot able to hunt its food, the legs were adopted to do circus not to hunt for its food, it was without food for these days it becoming week day by day. After the next 15 days it was died.

Tiger was living with freedom while it was in the forest, when it was trapped to work in circus, it duplicated to work like a cat, and unknowingly it adopted the nature & attitude of the cat, it lost its freedom of hunting an freedom of eating; it was trained to eat on time without hunting. The tiger was getting the food on time, but it lost the freedom.

In the same way, the job is to be considered as trap for income, the employee will be getting the income on time every month, but the freedom of living will be unknowingly lost by him. He will be getting the income on time, but there will be no time in his life to spend with that money. Job make us to Lose the freedom, to sell our time, like a trapped tiger and it makes the cat.

Life without freedom of time & money is not a complete & fulfilled life. The incomplete and un-fulfilled life is an ordinary life. Don't remain as ordinary man. Create a masterpiece life with your thinking.

44

The Billionaire Formula

"Every man needs women when his life is a mess, as a dream drives his life to success & a Queen protects the kind in chess"

Unlike generation assets holders, self made billionaires are thinkers or concept understanding masterpieces. Earning money is only based on A DEAL, HOW you can deal others? Dealings are based on either product or service (time).

The money transaction is done only with a deal, for product or service/time between peoples! You don't pay money to anyone unless you get some product or their service in the form of time, efforts, knowledge, information or idea.

Dealing is of 3 types

- ✓ Ordinary dealing
- ✓ Millionaire dealing
- ✓ Billionaire dealing

Based on HOW you are dealing the peoples you can be remaining as a poor or Ordinary, As Millionaire and As Billionaire;

Your income or wealth status will be based on your dealing, what kind of deal you are doing with the people;

Ordinary dealing

It's also called as limited or direct dealing; the man deals with peoples directly with his product or service, he can reach very limited peoples in a day, because human time is limited & fixed in a day, when this man is living based on his own time and dealing directly he can't move beyond his possibilities, so he remains poor or ordinary;

The work of an ordinary was based on time; the deal of time was selling his time for money. The direct dealing or time selling for money is limited to his efforts and limited available time in reaching more number of deals per day! The income is not only based on the size of deal, but number of deals a man can do directly in his limited time!

Example: a job doing employee, and self employment under his shutter; comes in this categories

Millionaire Dealing

It's also called as multiple dealing or indirect dealing;

A millionaire will never deal directly with the people; he creates a platform or a system, that platform will deal with the people. A Millionaire ill never deal directly, the organization under a millionaire will make them to deal with number of peoples in a limited time, and here the deal will be with number of peoples by number of employees under a millionaire on his platform;

The dealing was ineffective with the time, the time is limited for the millionaire too, but the deals are not limited for him, because the organization, platform, employees under him etc all, will deal with more number of peoples. As the organization deals with more number of peoples, the more wealth can be earned by the millionaire!

The time is limited to all, so the millionaire's dealing will be not limited to time, its limited to efforts of their organization size, which can be increased in many time exponentially.

The exponential increasing of team can increase the exponential increase of wealth!

Example: A business owner, an entrepreneur and Multi-Level-marketing or network marketing business.

Billionaire dealing

Billionaire deals with peoples through their ideas & thoughts; they don't deal with peoples directly, but they deal with their thoughts like an impact;

The billionaire deals with thoughts and those thoughts will deal with all the people of the world! The thoughts have infinite power unlike the ordinary and millionaire deal, they were limited to time & an effort, but the billionaire dealing is Infinity.

Example: They are the founders of companies and systems; Jeff Bezos was the founder & CEO of Amazon.com richest man in modern History. His thought was dealing with peoples through Amazon in serving them number of products;

Unlike becoming billionaires by generations of assets, majority of the Self made billionaires were thinkers, they deal with the world through their ideas and thoughts;

One formula, knowing to deal with world through ideas or thoughts is the 1st step of becoming a masterpiece; thinking about an idea or formula is the 2nd step of becoming a masterpiece; the final stage is bringing the idea to reality, which makes a man to stand as A masterpiece to the world, and world gives him success along with billion dollars!

Formula of Billionaire

"Ordinary deals with people directly with his time or effort in selling; a millionaire deals with infinity people through a platform in a form of product or service; A Billionaire deals with infinity peoples through his Ideas and thoughts";

Billionaire deals example:

    A thought of Jeff Bezos - Amazon

    A thought of Steve Jobs - I phone;

    A thought of Elon Musk – Tesla, SpaceX

    Yours _____?

"Billionaires deals with infinity number of peoples, but they never deal with people directly; they deal with their ideas & thoughts; think like a masterpiece and deal with the world through your Idea"!

What I can give to this world?

I am not a giving mindset, I am selfish!

I don't give something which makes me poor,

I don't give something which makes me to feel worry,

I don't give something which makes me to destroy self;

> I am a taking person, I don't give anything to this world,
>
> Because, I am selfish to make all human race out suffering;
>
> I can't change their lives by helping them in feeding stomach,
>
> I can't change their life by giving money to all, which can be over,
>
> I can't lift them on my shoulders, because I am not enough to lift the world on my shoulders,

What can I give something which can help them really to get benefited and getting a great lifestyle does my food, or my opportunity or money or my support?

NO

I can't change the lives of peoples by giving anything except one thing which can initiate them to think, to push them to work and hold them till achieving the greatness in all the possible way!

I can give only one thing to the world; I can give to the entire human Race!

MY THOUGHT

This makes human race to think!

Thank You

— Dr. San Bharath

Twitter: @drsanbharath

Tumblr: @drsanbharath

Instagram: @drsanbharath

Gmail: drsanbharath@gmail.com

For getting financial freedom

Website details: **www.rrff.co.in**

&

Whatsapp details: **995 108 7284**

www.ingramcontent.com/pod-product-compliance
Lightning Source LLC
Chambersburg PA
CBHW020734180526
45163CB00001B/240